CUMBRIA LIBRARIES
3 8003 04434 6146

D1621241

Cumbria County Library
Carlisle Group H.Q.
The Lanes
CARLISLE
CA3 8NX

GREAT WAR

THE COUNTDOWN TO GLOBAL CONFLICT

© Haynes Publishing, 2014

The right of Ian Welch to be identified as the author of this Work has
been asserted by him in accordance with the Copyright, Designs & Patents Act 1988.

All rights reserved. No part of this publication may be reproduced, stored in a retrieval system or transmitted, in any form or by any means, electronic, mechanical, photocopying, recording or otherwise, without prior permission in writing from the publisher.

First published in 2014

A catalogue record for this book is available from the British Library

ISBN: 978-0-85733-205-9

Published by Haynes Publishing, Sparkford, Yeovil,
Somerset BA22 7JJ, UK
Tel: 01963 442030 Fax: 01963 440001
Int. tel: +44 1963 442030 Int. fax: +44 1963 440001
E-mail: sales@haynes.co.uk
Website: www.haynes.co.uk

Haynes North America Inc., 861 Lawrence Drive,
Newbury Park, California 91320, USA

Images © Mirrorpix

Creative Director: Kevin Gardner
Designed for Haynes by BrainWave

Printed and bound in the US

GREAT WAR

THE COUNTDOWN TO GLOBAL CONFLICT

Ian Welch

LORD ROBERTS MESSAGE
"BE A CREDIT TO YOURSELF
AND TO THE NATION"

Introduction

The political tensions of the late 19th and early 20th century exploded in the middle of 1914 in a way that no one had ever before witnessed and the scale of which few could have predicted. The assassination of Archduke Francis Ferdinand and his wife at Sarajevo on 28th June led to a breakdown in relations between Austria-Hungary and Servia (now known as Serbia) that culminated in the former making a declaration of war a month later. The two countries had been on the brink of hostilities six years earlier after Austria-Hungary's annexation of Bosnia and Herzegovina that closely followed Bulgaria's declaration of independence.

Promises of support – or at least an assurance that certain acts would not bring retribution – were made and numerous treaties had been signed, sometimes decades earlier, between numerous countries who were thus obligated to defend their allies' borders. Within a matter of weeks, Europe was at war as the first truly global conflict gathered pace.

The chain of events that led to the First World War was not immediately obvious to the average person on the streets as – in the days before television, rolling news or the use of radio as an entertainment and communication medium – there was only one way for people to hear about what was happening . . . from reading the daily papers. Through the remarkable *Daily Mirror* archive, we reveal the key factors in the outbreak of the First World War in a way that brings the era to life and reveals much that has been lost to the mists of time.

Owing to the physical constraints of this publication, the exhaustive manifesto of events that triggered the First World War cannot be examined in infinite detail and it has not been possible to reproduce every word printed by the *Daily Mirror* that relates to these incidents. Where possible, we have highlighted the major issues – such as the Bosnian Crisis of 1908 and the Balkan Wars of 1912–13 (for which only the beginning and end are covered) – but are unable to include every detail.

On 7 August 1914 the first British troops – 120,000 highly trained members of the regular Army formed the British Expeditionary Force (BEF) commanded by Field Marshal John French – landed in Europe. They had been deployed in response to the German invasion of Belgium which violated the Treaty of London (1839) and forced the British to declare war on Germany. German Chancellor Theobald von Bethmann-Hollweg expressed his disbelief that the two countries would be going to war over a mere "scrap of paper," while many believed that the hostilities would be finished before Christmas. But the die had been cast for the most destructive and deadliest conflict the world had ever seen.

British soldiers with pack horses and donkeys watching enemy aircraft dropping bombs in 1916.

A Mk.1 tank in action in November 1916.

Whatever technological advances took place, the overriding image that we all hold in our minds of the Great War is one of men in trenches. These Canadian soldiers are on the Western Front in July 1916.

Advances in the weapons of war meant a more deadly battlefield than military commanders had historically been accustomed to.

Contrary to the belief of many, the First World War was not over by Christmas 1914 and the death toll mounted on an unparalleled scale.

Wounded British soldiers taken on board the hospital ship *Pegasus*, November 1914.

A wounded British soldier waiting for the Red Cross and a train home in time for the first Christmas of the war, 1914.

Members of the BEF wounded in some of the first encounters with the German Army in France, seen here in the drawing room of the Southern General Hospital, Bournbrook, recovering from their wounds in November 1914.

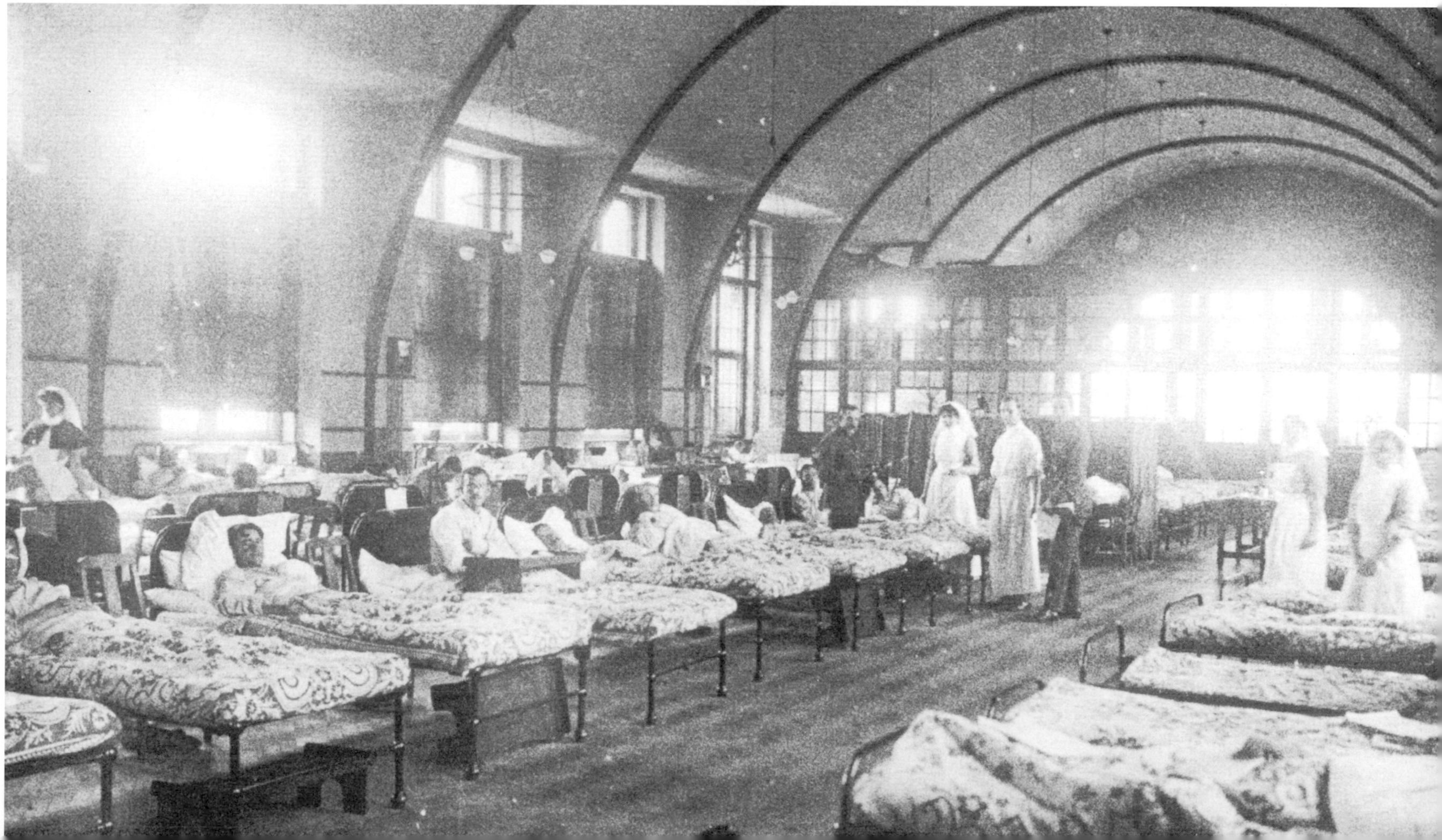

17 December 1903 saw the Wright Brothers – Orville and Wilbur – make their first successful controlled, powered and sustained, heavier-than-air human flight to announce mankind's arrival in the skies. Their original machine of 1903, in which they first flew, was damaged by high winds in Ohio and was never used again. This Wright Brothers plane was flown in Pau, France, 1909.

Development in aviation was slow to begin with, but as with all wars it pushed the boundaries of technology. Here in 1914 airmen simply drop their bombs.

▲ A Sopwith Camel, barely recognisable from the Wright Brothers' aircraft. This was one of the Royal Flying Corps' most successful fighters in the First World War.

◀ By 1915 aircraft were dropping torpedoes to try to sink enemy shipping.

Contents

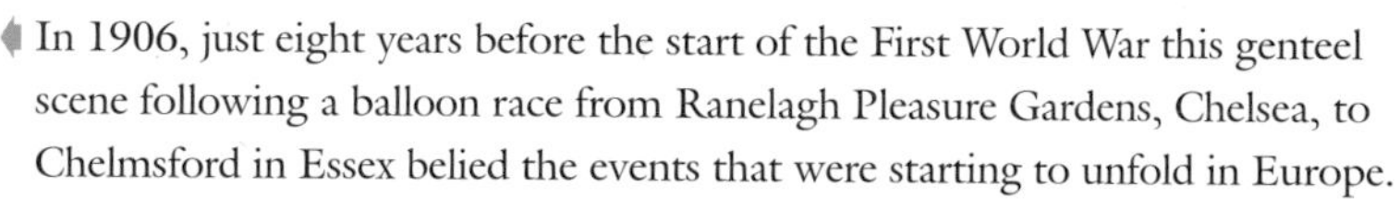

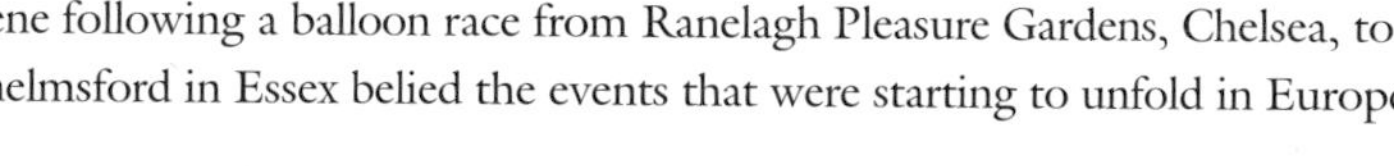

In 1906, just eight years before the start of the First World War this genteel scene following a balloon race from Ranelagh Pleasure Gardens, Chelsea, to Chelmsford in Essex belied the events that were starting to unfold in Europe.

Tensions Rise as the New Century Dawns

December **1904** – 8 December **1908**

While one prominent writer debated whether it would be an Anglo-Saxon or Slavic nation that would rise to dominate Europe, tensions in the Balkans were being placed under increasing pressure with Bulgaria's declaration of independence and Austria's annexation of Bosnia and Herzegovina.

For a while after declaring their independence in 1908, it looked as though Bulgaria would have to defend its newly formed kingdom. The Principality of Bulgaria had been divided under the Treaty of Berlin in 1878.

2 December **1904**

THE FUTURE EMPIRE OF THE WORLD

IS IT TO BE ANGLO-SAXON OR RUSSIAN?

AN AMERICAN AUTHOR'S PLEA – SLAV OR SAXON

by W D Foulke

A book of particular interest at the present time. The author holds that the great struggle of the future is to be between the Anglo-Saxons and the Slavs – that is, between the English-speaking nations and Russia.

England and Russia are the two great colonising countries, and they are bound to come into conflict sooner or later. Russia is continually expanding her dominions in Asia – the present war with Japan was caused by her endeavours to obtain possession of Manchuria and Korea: and those endeavours are but the preliminary steps to the Russification of China. Listen to this quotation from the "Sviet", a Russian newspaper:

"The East, with all its countries, as China, Balochistan, and even India, is by the will of Providence destined for the Russian people."

If the Russians ever secure China, says Mr Foulke, they will go on to India. Russia will become the mistress of Asia, and then Asia will begin the conquest of Europe. "There is absolutely no possibility of resisting Russian aggression," says Mr Foulke, "unless the work is commenced at an early day," and he urges the United States to be ready to commence it with Great Britain whenever the time comes.

What would be the result if Russia became the paramount power of the world? The answer is: look at the methods Russia employs to govern those who have the misfortune to be her subjects now.

The Russians themselves are liable to exile to Siberia, sometimes on mere suspicion and without a trial, and to have their houses invaded by the police and their property searched without a reason given. The unfortunate nations Russia has conquered are in a far worse position. The Poles are not allowed to teach their own language in their own schools; in Armenia the national church has been abolished; whilst the Jews are treated worse in Russia today than they were in Western Europe in the Middle Ages.

In short, the Russian system of government is barbarous. It would be a fearful blow to the progress of civilisation if in the great struggle that is to come the Slav should overcome the Saxon.

9 March **1906**

CHEAPER AND BETTER ARMY

SWEEPING SCHEME OF THE NEW WAR MINISTER

Mr Haldane, the Secretary for War, made his first important pronouncement of military policy in the House of Commons last night.

The main features of his masterly exposition, delivered largely without the assistance of notes, and occupying two hours and five minutes in delivery, were the following:

1 A declaration for more efficiency at a less expenditure.
2 A reference to the rise of a new school of thinking officers since the South African war.
3 A wish that the nations of the world would take council together to reduce armaments.
4 Estimates only £17,000 less than last year.
5 A condemnation of the policy of borrowing for military work.
6 A declaration that the present Government intended to "pay their way".

"A three months' tenure of office," said Mr Haldane, "is too short a time to enable me to produce a new Army scheme." Nevertheless, the Minister entertained the House to his ideas on military reform.

The following decisions, he announced, had been arrived at:

- The ammunition stores, constructed for the defence of London, are to disappear, root and branch.

- Some 300 guns, for defence purposes, at various points around the coast are to be swept away.

- Some Colonial garrisons will be reduced to correspond with the new naval policy.

The system of making continuous reconnaissances of positions in this country, with the view of defending us against a foreign enemy, will be stopped.

After a frank confession that "the path of a War Minister was strewn with difficulties," Mr Haldane drew attention to the enormous expenditure on the Army not merely by this nation, but by other Powers in a corresponding position.

COST OF OTHER ARMIES

"German military expenditure has risen in 11 years by 25 per cent, and stands at £31,000,000 against our £30,000,000. French military expenditure stands at £29,000,000.

"I have found my task a fascinating one," admitted the Minister, "and I have tried to put my finger on the spot where the sources of the present expenditure lay.

"The Government is pledged to economy, and I have scanned the Estimates with a view of discovering how much can be eliminated without any sacrifice of efficiency."

The reason that the present Estimates were only £17,000 less than those of last year was due to the automatic increases in cost on various branches of the service amounting to £780,000.

"Having that large sum to get rid of," he explained, "I consulted with the Army Council, and with their valuable expert aid I have succeeded in getting the Estimates for the coming year reduced, and I am assured that there will be no diminution of efficiency."

LESSONS OF THE WAR

With much eloquence, accompanied by convincing gesture, the Minister submitted that the Army ought to be so organised that it could respond at once to conditions of policy so that it could be expanded or diminished as occasion required.

The lessons of the South African war had been learned, and he did not think the Army was ever more efficient than it was at the present time.

"The British Army is wanted for service oversea, and it is necessarily a professional force. It must," said Mr Haldane, "be of that high quality which cannot be obtained by conscription."

A roar of Ministerial cheers followed this declaration.

"The Army must be of strictly limited dimensions. The size of the force must depend on policy, and I wish the nations of the world would take counsel together to reduce armaments, the burden of which is pressing on every civilised nation."

An interesting suggestion followed. Dealing with the question of expansion and the powers of the auxiliary forces, Mr Haldane said he would like to see more men voluntarily take upon themselves "the elements of some military training".

"I do not see why people should not shoot with the rifle as well as play with the football."

In the case of war, given the skeleton organisation, there would be a possibility of expanding the defensive forces and training them to the necessary standard of efficiency before they had to take the field.

"We should dismiss from our minds all notion of organising ourselves up to a war standard in a time of peace," he urged.

His ideas could be worked out by means of a devolution of military administration to local governing units.

MAKE PEACE A CERTAINTY

With such an organisation no war would be entered upon without the full assent of the people.

"A nation under arms in that fashion would be a nation under arms for the sake of peace. With such an organisation at home it would be possible to reduce the striking force and effect economies on a large scale.

"If the Colonies followed suit," submitted the Minister, "the Empire might raise potential forces of a character which would make peace a certainty for generations to come."

25 May **1908**

PIGEONS OUSTED BY "WIRELESS"

500 BIRDS SOLD OUT OF THE NAVAL SERVICE YESTERDAY

Five hundred of the best carrier pigeons in the world were offered for sale yesterday afternoon at Messrs Hollingsworth's auction rooms in Holborn. The birds, which were in splendid condition, were from the naval lofts at Gibraltar and Sheerness, which are being disestablished owing to the perfecting of wireless technology. All the best-known fanciers in the South of England were present, attracted by the opportunity of purchasing such excellent birds.

Every "homer" in the cages boasted a long pedigree, and, what was more important, was a "stayer". With the exception of a small number of young birds which had not been flown, the distance covered was noted in the catalogue, the majority having from 120 to 150 sea miles to their credit.

Lieutenant W Barrett, RN, watched the sale on behalf of the Admiralty, and the auctioneer was Mr T May, who established the successful pigeon post in South Africa during the late Boer War at the time when our lines of communication could not always be depended upon.

DISPLACED BY WIRELESS

The reason for the Admiralty disposing of the birds is to be found in the agreement with the Marconi Wireless Telegraphy Company, and in the elements of the Berlin International Wireless Telegraphy Convention of 1906, which comes into force on 1 July next.

◆ Guglielmo Marconi, inventor of the wireless.

◆ Far from being replaced by the wireless, carrier pigeons would continue to be a useful military asset for decades to come. Here a French Army officer prepares a carrier pigeon to carry a message back to headquarters in August 1914.

Under the provisions of the convention it is secured that as many as possible of the shore stations of the world shall be established on British territory. The effect of this is that in time of war England would be in a position of immense advantage as regards wireless communication both with the ships of the Royal Navy and the mercantile fleets. The Admiralty therefore feels that the time has come when the carrier pigeons may be dispensed with, and yesterday's auction was the result of that opinion.

Nevertheless, it was freely stated amongst those present, who were in the best position to know, that a large number of the pick of the birds had been bought by agents acting for Germany.

The naval pigeon service had been established for 12 years, and during that time the weaker birds were systematically eliminated.

Naturally their buyers will be unable to fly them for the reason that the moment one of them was liberated it would make straight for either Gibraltar or Sheerness, according to which dockyard it came from. On the other hand, they are capital pairs from which to breed.

The range of a carrier pigeon is enormous. During the recent flyings birds flew from San Sebastian, in Spain, to England – a distance of 700 odd miles – and one bird, whose loft was in the north of the country, achieved the remarkable result of 830 miles.

In connection with this sale, many well-informed people are of the opinion that were there a war the Government would greatly regret disposing of the lofts, and would be forced to recommence the pigeon service, no system of telegraphy being sufficiently immune from tapping.

15 August **1908**

BRITISH AIRSHIP

NEW ARMY DIRIGIBLE MAKES A SUCCESSFUL TRIP AT ALDERSHOT

A short but highly successful trial trip was made over Aldershot yesterday evening by the new Army dirigible war balloon. For 20 minutes the airship circled the air over the common, ascending and descending in wide and narrow circles, and at speeds varying from 10 to 20 miles per hour.

A short straight flight against the wind was tried and then, in narrowing circles, the airship was brought down by means of its apparatus until within 150 foot from the ground. Then the engines were stopped and a little gas allowed to escape, to bring tow ropes within reach of the towing parties, who quickly brought the car down to the level of the ground.

A few bright flashes were observable while in the air from the engines, but one of the experts stated there was no danger of igniting the gas in the balloon.

On reaching the ground, the airship was towed back to its shed in safety.

Known officially as Dirigible No 2, the airship made, after two ineffectual attempts to start, a successful circular voyage on 24 July last. On that occasion Colonel Capper, who directed operations, expressed himself as "quite satisfied" with the progress made by the war balloon.

Dirigibles were a threat to enemy forces over both land and sea.

2 September **1908**

"AM I A JINGO?"

Mr Robert Blatchford, the well-known socialist writer, whose articles in the *Clarion* on the danger of a German invasion have aroused considerable attention.

5 October 1908

"TSAR OF THE BULGARIANS"

DANGER OF WAR

Bulgaria's action in taking over the control of a section of the Oriental Railway is precipitating a crisis in the Balkans which may lead to a war between that country and Turkey.

Bulgaria is determined not to give up her control of the railway, and it is believed that today Prince Ferdinand will proclaim himself Tsar of the Bulgarians. In this he would have his people solid behind him.

Bulgaria, however, is only half the present problem. President Fallières has received a letter from the Austrian Emperor which is believed to state quite definitely Austria's intention to formally annex Bosnia and Herzegovina which, though administered since 1878 by Austria-Hungary, are still nominally Turkish.

Last night it was learned in London that the British Government is making efforts to secure peace and Turkey, at the insistence of England, has agreed to make concessions to Bulgaria on the railway question which may avoid extreme measures.

In Paris yesterday the gravest fears were entertained, and there was a constant coming and going at the Foreign Office.

TODAY'S ANNOUNCEMENT

(from our own correspondent)

Paris, 4 October – I have the best authority for stating that tomorrow Prince Ferdinand of Bulgaria will proclaim the national independence of his country. The proclamation will be made at Tirnovo, the ancient capital of Bulgaria, and the Prince will proclaim himself a Sovereign Independent Prince, under the title of Tsar of the Bulgarians.

In spite of official silence it is an open secret that France was informed on Friday of Prince Ferdinand's intention to make the proclamation tomorrow. It is further known that in an autograph letter to President Fallières the Emperor Frances Joseph announces his intention to proclaim shortly the annexation to the Austrian Empire of Bosnia and Herzegovina, which will constitute a parallel act to the declaration of independence.

The utmost official apprehension exists in Paris at the dangerous policy of Austria and Bulgaria, which means the tearing up of the Treaty of Berlin.

It is considered here that, if it is not already too late, France, Russia and Great Britain should combine to take up the cause of Turkey and bring about the immediate meeting of an international conference to constitute a new Charter, assuring some kind of political stability.

It is certain that, in view of the violation of Turkey's rights, she is entitled to substantial compensation. Only a sound understanding between France, Great Britain and Russia – a triple alliance – and the energetic, combined action of these three nations can prevent war.

BULGARIAN MINISTERS ASSEMBLE

Sofia, 4 October – All the Ministers have gone to Rustchuk, where they will await the arrival of Prince Ferdinand on his return from abroad.

It is stated that the Prince will preside at a Council of Ministers at Rustchuk, at which very important decisions will be arrived at relative to the Oriental Railway and the Gueshoff incidents, and it is hinted that in the case of a divergence in the opinions of the Prince and the Ministers a dismissal of the Cabinet is not impossible.

AMBASSADOR'S OPINION

Vienna, 4 October – Nizanie Pasha, the new Turkish Ambassador in Berlin, who is passing through Vienna on his way to Berlin, in an interview published by the *Neue Freie Presse*, declares that Turkey will never consent to Bulgaria declaring herself independent, but he does not think that the Oriental Railway dispute will lead to war.

For the present, both countries must wait for the decision of the Powers signatory to the Berlin Treaty.

ANNEXATION MUST COME

Vienna, 4 October – The semi-official *Neue Freie Presse* asserts that the Emperor Francis Joseph, in the autograph letter he has sent to President Fallières, refers to the necessity of changing the present relations between the occupied provinces of Bosnia and Herzegovina and the Monarchy, but adds that the change contemplated will not overstep the limits of the Berlin Treaty.

In a leading article it points out that annexation is not the only method of convincing the Bosnian people and outsiders that the provinces will never more be separated from the Monarchy, and declares that it will not be difficult to find within the limits of the Berlin Treaty a title of ownership which will have a strong effect upon the Bosnians while avoiding diplomatic complications.

The article continues: "For the present the world may learn that we shall never abandon Bosnia and that we shall annex it, though the time cannot yet be stated."

The *Neue Freie Presse* does not believe that Great Britain will oppose Austria's policy regarding Bosnia, as it was the British

statesmen of the Victorian era who led and even drove Austria into Bosnia, but should even an old friendship be entirely forgotten, the pillars, it says, on which the power of the Monarchy rests in Bosnia cannot be overturned.

BRITAIN'S EFFORTS FOR PEACE

It is understood that the British Government have made proposals to the Turkish and Bulgarian Governments with a view to a settlement of the question of the Oriental Railway.

The Turkish Government readily agreed that, in the event of the railway being temporarily restored to the company, they would consent to the lease being transferred from the company to the Bulgarian Government, the rights of the Porte being duly safeguarded.

The British Government have urged the signatory Powers of the Treaty of Berlin to recommend this solution to the Sofia Government, with a view to a return to the normal state of affairs. It is understood that the Great Powers have agreed to act accordingly.

CAUSE OF THE TROUBLE

The present crisis is really the outcome of the strong movement in Bulgaria for complete independence, and the bid for the control of that part of the Oriental Railway which traverses Eastern Rumelia was a step towards that end.

By the Berlin Treaty of 1878 Bulgaria was made a principality under the suzerainty of Turkey. The Oriental Railway is the property of Turkey, and is leased to a company under German and Austrian control. The lease expires in 1958, and the whole railway then reverts to Turkey.

The excuse given by the Bulgarian Government for the occupation of the line was that a strike had disorganised the working. When the strike was over, however, Bulgaria refused to withdraw its troops, which were guarding the line. Turkey has the support of all the Powers in the dispute, with the exception of Austria, which is credited with supporting Bulgaria's aims in order to cover her own annexation of Bosnia and Herzegovina.

These two provinces, with a population of 1,737,000 all told, were taken from immediate Turkish control by the Berlin Treaty, and have since been occupied and administered by Austria-Hungary. Strictly, however, Bosnia and Herzegovina are still Turkish provinces.

ARMIES OF TURKEY AND BULGARIA

The Bulgarian Army has in peace a strength of about 60,000 men. The total war strength is about 380,000 men, and it is expected that an organised field army of 210,000, with 500 guns, could be massed on the Turkish frontier in 10 days.

The peace strength of the Turkish Army is about 230,000 men, with 1,200 guns, or whom 152,000 men and 990 guns are in Europe. Its nominal war strength is 1,100,000 men, but the Turkish mobilisation, however, is slow and would require six or eight weeks.

6 October 1908

BULGARIA CLAIMS INDEPENDENCE

GRAVE BALKAN CRISIS

The crisis in the Balkans came to a head by the proclamation of Prince Ferdinand as the Tsar of Bulgaria at Tirnovo, the ancient capital.

It is now known also that on one day this week (probably Thursday) Austria-Hungary will carry out her intention, conveyed to the Powers by Emperor Francis Joseph in an autograph letter, of annexing Bosnia and Herzegovina.

The situation is thus complicated, and though the decisions of Bulgaria and of Austria-Hungary are separate in themselves, they both violate the Treaty of Berlin and, coming together, increase the danger and difficulty.

In Constantinople, the news of Prince Ferdinand's proclamation, though not unexpected, was received with consternation, and a meeting of the Cabinet was held last night to consider the situation. Turkey is adopting a conciliatory attitude, and it is hoped in Constantinople that it will not be necessary to go to war.

The situation, however, is alarming and from Vienna comes a report that the Bulgarian Army has followed the proclamation of independence by marching on the Turkish frontier. The Turkish Army is moving to meet the advancing Bulgarians, and in Austria a rapid mobilisation of troops is taking place.

It is stated on the best authority that the British Government views the action of Bulgaria with extreme disfavour. His Majesty's Government cannot admit the right of any Power to alter an international treaty with the consent of the other parties to it and they will, therefore, refuse to sanction any infraction of the Berlin Treaty and decline to recognise what has been done until the views of the other Powers are known, especially those of Turkey, who is more directly concerned than anyone else.

Russia, France and Italy are in complete harmony with Great

The Daily Mirror

THE MORNING JOURNAL WITH THE SECOND LARGEST NET SALE.

No. 1,541. Registered at the G. P. O. as a Newspaper. TUESDAY, OCTOBER 6, 1908. One Halfpenny.

WAR CRISIS IN THE NEAR EAST: INDEPENDENCE OF BULGARIA PROCLAIMED: THE FIRST TSAR OF THE BULGARIANS AND HIS CONSORT.

Events in the Near East yesterday reached a crisis as the result of which all Europe may be involved in an extremely complicated situation. Bulgaria, which since the Berlin Treaty of 1878 has ranked as a tributary principality under the suzerainty of the Sultan of Turkey, was proclaimed an independent nation in the ancient capital of Tirnovo. This momentous step was taken in the presence of Prince Ferdinand, who has been on the throne of Bulgaria since 1887, and it is stated that he will take the title of Tsar of the Bulgarians. The gravity of the situation is accentuated by the fact that Austria will [illegible] announce the formal annexation of Bosnia and Herzegovina. Thus two provisions of the Treaty of Berlin will have been contravened, and the action of the remaining signatories of the Treaty remains problematical.

Britain in the crisis. It has been suggested that an international conference should be held for a fresh settlement of affairs in the Balkans.

On the other hand, Germany, according to reports from Berlin, is prepared to support Austria "through thick and thin" in the annexation of Bosnia and Herzegovina.

Count Mensdorff, the Austro-Hungarian Ambassador, has left London for Balmoral to lay before His Majesty the King the autograph letter of the Emperor Francis Joseph with regard to Bosnia and Herzegovina. His Majesty's Government has received a notification from the Austrian Government of its intentions with respect to the occupied provinces.

7 October **1908**

AUSTRIA ANNEXES PROVINCES

EMPEROR'S PROCLAMATION TO BOSNIA-HERZEGOVINA

The formal annexation by Austria of Bosnia and Herzegovina will take place today. In a rescript, to be published in an official Vienna paper today, the Emperor Francis Joseph announces that he has extended his sovereignty over the two provinces, until now nominally Turkish, although administered by Austria since 1878.

At the same time, the Emperor has ordered the evacuation by his troops of the adjoining Turkish district of Novi Bazar, occupied by them since 1879.

Servia is in a wild ferment over the annexation of Bosnia and Herzegovina which, she claims, will menace her national existence. The population of these provinces is to a large extent Servian. Reserves to the number of 120,000 have been called on to join the Servian Army.

The danger of war between Turkey and Bulgaria has diminished, and Turkey has signified her intention of appealing to the Powers before adopting extreme measures. A Circular Note will be addressed to the Powers pointing out the necessity of taking measures to secure the observance of the Berlin Treaty.

In case of necessity, however, Turkey will defend her rights by force; and presumably it will be necessary for her to do so should she fail to obtain redress from the Powers.

Meanwhile, it is now practically certain that an international conference will be held and the representatives of Britain, France and Russia had several meetings in Paris yesterday.

16 October **1908**

CONFERENCE ON BALKAN CRISIS

BRITAIN AND RUSSIA AGREE OF PLANS FOR A SETTLEMENT

It was officially announced in London last night that Britain and Russia had agreed that an international conference was necessary for the settlement of the questions raised by Bulgaria's declaration of independence and Austria-Hungary's annexation of Bosnia and Herzegovina.

This Conference, the official statement says, should confine itself to dealing with the questions arising out of the recent violations of the Treaty of Berlin. Its objects should be:

- The compensation of Turkey and the strengthening of the new regime there.
- The satisfaction of the legitimate desires of the smaller Balkan Powers, but not at the expense of Turkey.

The Cretan question is provisionally excluded from the scope of the Conference as being a matter for the four protecting Powers. The question of the Dardanelles is not to be raised, this being considered a matter for Russia and Turkey, the two Powers directly concerned.

19 October **1908**

WAR IN BALKANS NARROWLY AVERTED

BULGARIA GIVES WAY TO TURKEY'S DEMANDS

Within the last two days Turkey and Bulgaria have been within an ace of war, but at the 11th hour Bulgaria gave way and it now seems unlikely that the peace of Europe will be disturbed.

Alarmed by Bulgaria's military preparations, Turkey decided to take immediate steps to protect herself from any incursion from Bulgaria. Rolling stock was got ready to convey reinforcements to the troops in Anatolia, on the Bulgarian frontier, reservists were called to the flag, arms and ammunition were hurriedly got ready, and preparations made for the dispatch of heavy guns.

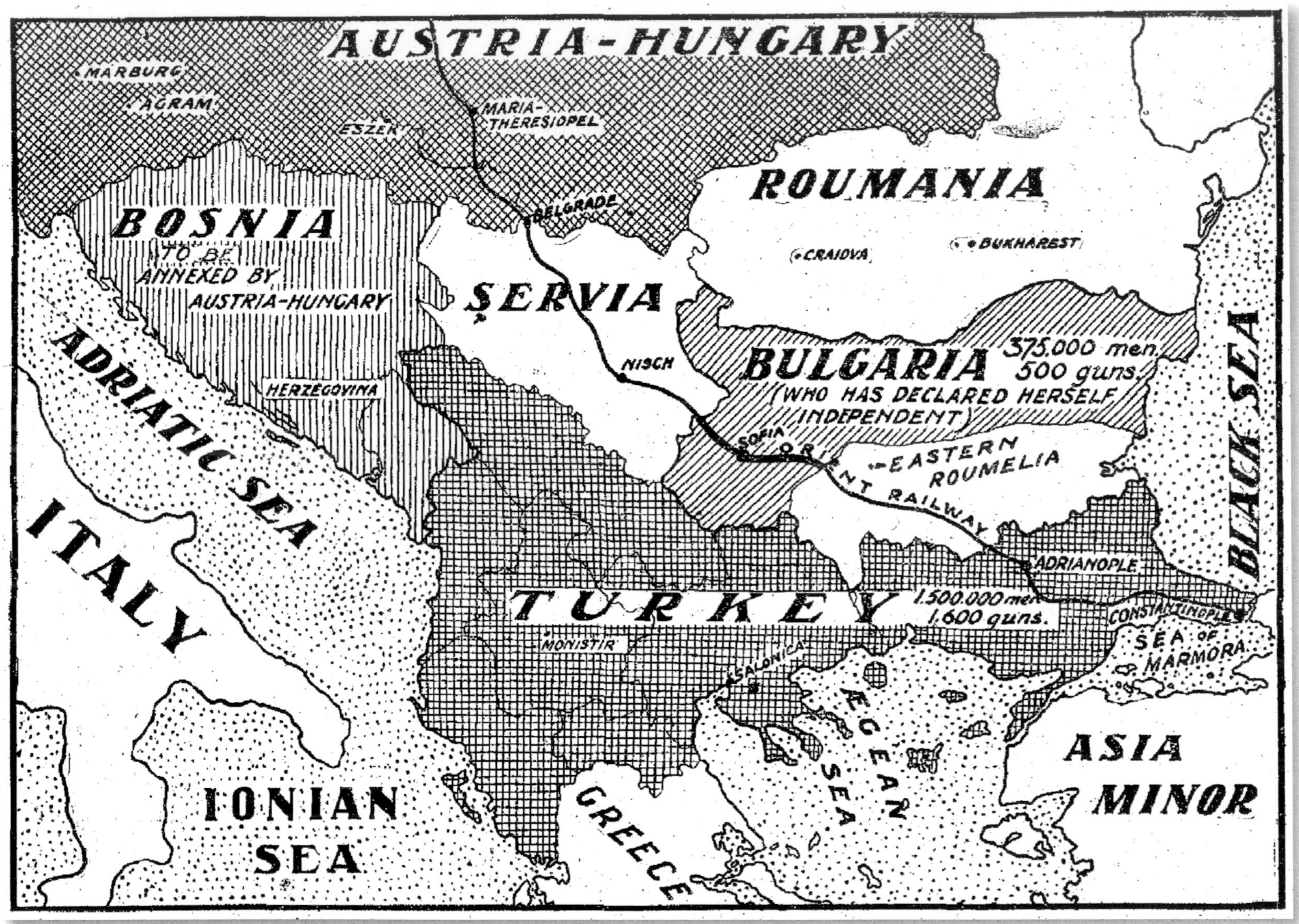

AUSTRIA-HUNGARY
MARBURG
AGRAM
ESZEK
MARIA-THERESIOPEL
ROUMANIA
BOSNIA
TO BE ANNEXED BY AUSTRIA-HUNGARY
BELGRADE
CRAIOVA
BUKHAREST
SERVIA
BULGARIA
375.000 men. 500 guns.
(WHO HAS DECLARED HERSELF INDEPENDENT)
NISCH
HERZEGOVINA
ADRIATIC SEA
SOFIA
ORIENT RAILWAY
EASTERN ROUMELIA
BLACK SEA
ITALY
ADRIANOPLE
TURKEY
1.500.000 men 1.600 guns.
CONSTANTINOPLE
SEA OF MARMORA
MONISTIR
SALONICA
AEGEAN SEA
ASIA MINOR
IONIAN SEA
GREECE

This was on Saturday, but last night the whole situation had undergone a radical change.

Finding that Turkey was in earnest, Bulgaria gave way to her demands, and immediately the Turkish preparations were stopped.

So hopeful is the outlook, states the Turkish Ambassador in Paris, that "within 48 hours events will be modified in a manner most favourable to the maintenance of peace."

Meanwhile the negotiations for the proposed international conference are progressing, though Germany does not entirely approve of the draft programme in the form in which it has been published.

BULGARIA GIVES WAY

Paris, 18 October – Within the last 24 hours Turkey and Bulgaria have been within an ace of going to war, but happily matters have been peacefully arranged, and it does not seem likely that peace will be disturbed.

The facts are these. Consequent on active Bulgarian military preparations of a threatening character, which were taking place on the Turkish frontier, the Turkish Government decided to take immediate steps to meet the possibility of a Bulgarian incursion into Turkish territory.

Fifty railway locomotives belonging to the Anatolian Railway were concentrated at Constantinople on Friday night, ready to rush forward as rapidly as possible 25,000 men to strengthen the army corps at Anatolia.

Telegraphic orders were issued calling up for tomorrow (Monday) morning 20,000 reservists residing in the immediate neighbourhood of Constantinople, the general officer commanding the 3rd Army Corps received orders to mobilise as quickly as possible five divisions, consisting of 80 battalions of 850 men each, and it was computed that within one week 161,000 troops would be in Anatolia.

One hundred and eight rapid-firing guns, 10 vans of Mauser rifles, and 15 wagons of ammunition were dispatched from Constantinople to the probable seat of war, and arrangements were being made for dispatch, on Monday next, of a part of the 200 heavy guns for the 3rd Army Corps.

It was noticed that none of the troops forming the Sultan's bodyguard, and consisting of 5,000 picked men, were included in the soldiers ordered to the front. Curiously enough, too, all those officers who took a prominent part in the Turkish Constitution had been ordered to the front.

Another strange fact is that whilst these preparations were kept as secret as possible, and Press telegrams referring to the subject were censured, alarmist telegrams were sent through the German Embassy to German newspapers.

It is obvious that the Sultan's party favours war as a means of destroying the Constitution, but the influence of the Young Turks is too strong to permit war unless it becomes inevitable.

This probably explains the statements made in Paris by Naoum Pasha, the Turkish Ambassador, who said this afternoon: "It is true that up to yesterday (Saturday) morning my Government was rapidly and silently mobilising for war, which seemed inevitable owing to Bulgarian provocations, but although this was true yesterday it was no longer so last night.

"What had happened meanwhile, I will tell you, Bulgaria, finding we were in grim earnest, gave us last evening the definite and full assurances for which we had asked.

"I must not tell what these assurances are, but immediately the Turkish Government had received them telegraphic orders were issued stopping all further preparations for Turkish mobilisation.

"Orders for calling up reserves were countermanded last night, the rushing of further supplies to the frontier was stopped, and within 48 hours events will be modified in a manner most favourable to the maintenance of peace."

300,000 TURKISH TROOPS FOR FRONTIER

Paris, 18 October – The *Figaro* publishes the following telegram from Constantinople, dated yesterday, 7.30pm: "The day has been troubled by serious fears of war, but a feeling of relief has been produced by better news from Sofia."

A telegram dated yesterday 7.00pm, published by the *Action*, says: "300,000 men will doubtless be sent to the frontier, in order to exercise pressure upon the diplomatic negotiations and upon the Conference."

The following telegram has been received here from Constantinople: "It is declared in Turkish semi-official circles that no orders have been given for the mobilisation of the Anatolian Army Corps. It is admitted, however, that measures have been taken for the transport of troops."

The *Petit Temps* publishes the following telegram from Constantinople, dispatched at 3.25 this afternoon: "In view of the reply sent by Bulgaria to the demand that she should relinquish the Oriental Railway, of which she had taken possession, the mobilisation of the Turkish Army was decided upon this morning."

BULGARIAN MOBILISATION

Paris, 17 October – The *Petit Parisien*'s Sofia correspondent telegraphs under yesterday's date: "According to information from a very trustworthy source, the mobilisation of the Bulgarian troops is being effected gradually, in very discreet manner, on the pretext of their being called out for training. If this fact is taken in conjunction with the telegrams regarding the Turkish preparations, the fears of a conflict may be regarded as serious."

AUSTRIAN TROOPS ON FRONTIER

Cettigne, 17 October – Austrian troops are massed not far from the southern frontier of Montenegro, and guns and war material have been sent to the Bocche di Cattaro.

In Government circles here these proceedings are regarded as provocation on the part of Austria-Hungary, and it is feared that they will also force Montenegro, where great irritation prevails, to mobilise her troops and to summon all Montenegrins abroad to the colours.

Paris, 18 October – A *New York Herald* telegram from Constantinople states that it is reported from a reliable source that Austria, in consequence of her protests to Turkey against boycotting being ineffective, decided upon a naval demonstration, but changed her mind immediately the British fleet appeared in Turkish waters.

23 October **1908**

AUSTRIA CUTS OFF WAR SUPPLIES

PASSAGE OF AMMUNITION TO SERVIA AND MONTENEGRO FORBIDDEN

News from the Near East yesterday was not reassuring, the preparations for war continuing in several States. Austria has taken the significant step of forbidding the export from or passage through her territory of war material for Servia and Montenegro.

This action is semi-officially attributed to her desire to avert a conflict in the Balkans, but its effect is to cut short the supplies of her possible antagonists. An indication of the tension of the situation in Servia is given by the arrest, under the impression that he was a spy, of *The Daily Mirror* staff photographer, while engaged in taking photographs from the frontier railway bridge across the River Save. After two hours' retention, however, he succeeded in proving his identity and was released.

CUTTING OFF SERVIA'S WAR SUPPLIES

Vienna, 22 October – The *Wiener Zeitung* publishes an ordinance of the Minister of Finance forbidding the export or passage through Austro-Hungarian territory of war material destined for Servia or Montenegro. The prohibition applies also to Bosnia and Herzegovina.

According to a semi-official communiqué, the order is to be attributed to the desire of the Austro-Hungarian Monarchy to avert any conflicts in the Balkan Peninsula.

Belgrade, 22 October – A body of students, professors and military officers this evening held a torchlight procession in honour of General Vukotitch, the Montenegrin envoy. Patriotic songs were sung and groans for Austria given.

The wrath against Austria-Hungary received a fresh impetus when the order was made known prohibiting the transport through the dual monarchy of war material for Servia.

AUSTRO-TURKISH AGREEMENT

Vienna, 22 October – In an apparently inspired communiqué, the *Neue Freie Presse* states that the negotiations between Austria-Hungary and Turkey have already reached the basis of an agreement, Turkey showing perfect willingness to recognise the annexation of Bosnia and Herzegovina.

The question of what compensation Austria should offer Turkey in return is now the subject of discussion between Constantinople and Vienna. The report that Austria would give Turkey a sort of guarantee for Turkey's territorial integrity in the Balkans, especially in the Sanjak of Novi Bazar, may prove true.

The Vienna Cabinet is acting in close connection with the Berlin Foreign Office, which is kept precisely informed of their progress. In diplomatic circles, however, it is reported that affairs in Constantinople are not proceeding so favourably for the Austrians as the foregoing would indicate.

OBJECT OF NEGOTIATIONS

In reply to questions addressed to him in the House of Commons yesterday Sir Edward Grey said that the negotiations now going on between the Powers were intended to secure agreement on a programme which would enable them to arrive at a settlement of the difficulties in the Near East.

As Turkey was the Power most adversely affected by what had taken place, the British Government trusted that the first object of the Powers would be to secure compensation to Turkey and to safeguard her interests. The approval of the Turkish Government was a necessary condition to the adoption of any programme, and as her views had not been expressed on the suggestions made he could make no further statement.

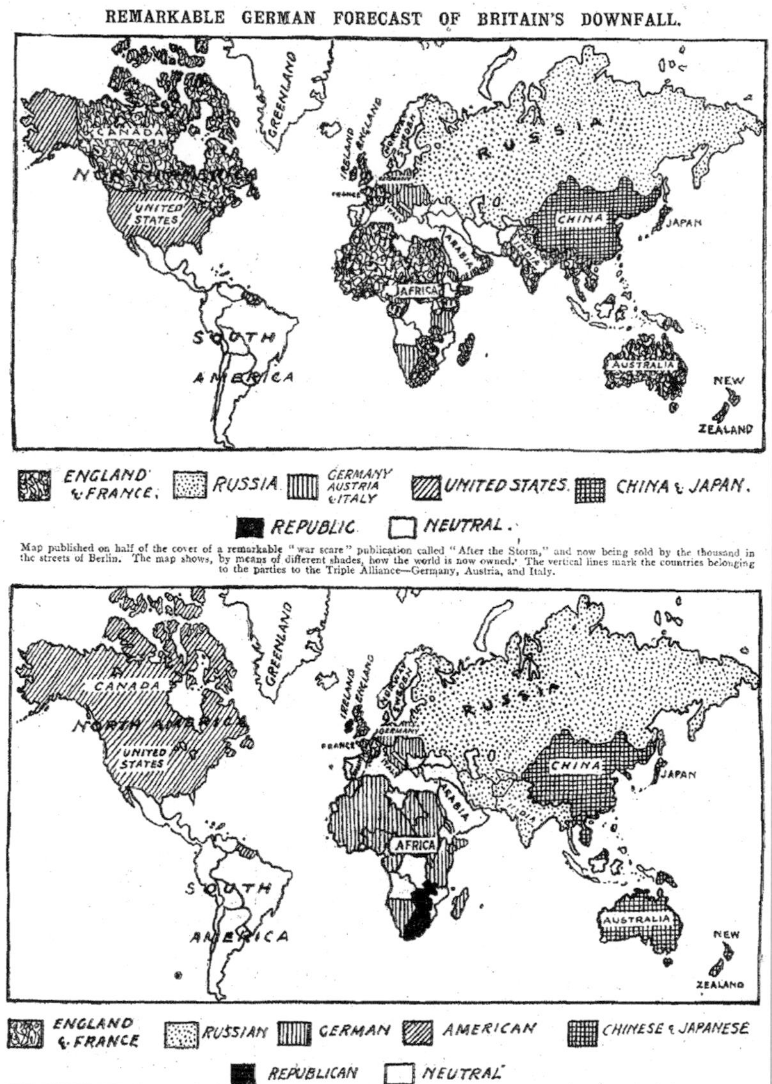

A German propaganda publication forecasting a change in the world's power struggle.

24 October **1908**

PEACE OR WAR IN THE BALKANS

TURKEY AND AUSTRIA

Despite the fact that gloomy rumours came from the Near East, and notably from Constantinople, during yesterday, the outlook last night was, on the whole, more satisfactory. The most disquieting factor in the situation was the attitude adopted by Bulgaria towards Turkey.

Bulgaria's demands are regarded by the latter Power as unreasonable, and her envoys have left Constantinople without having come to any definite settlement of the matters in dispute.

It was stated in Vienna yesterday that Turkey, acting under British influence, had broken off direct negotiations with Austria on the subject of Bosnia and Herzegovina.

Austria is resolved to maintain the position already taken, and only to attend a conference when the annexation of Bosnia and Herzegovina is registered as an accomplished fact. Germany supports Austria, and will take the same course.

26 October **1908**

SERVIA MOBILISES FIRST RESERVES

ATTACKS ON BRITAIN

Servia has ordered the mobilisation of her first line of reserves, and it is stated that further mobilisations are imminent. This step has been taken, it is stated, in consequence of the seizure by Austria of a Servian island in the frontier river, the Drina.

King Peter has publicly declared that an alliance had been concluded between Montenegro and Servia.

Britain meanwhile is the object of bitter attacks by the Austrian Press from the semi-official organs downwards.

She is accused of being responsible for the breaking off by Turkey of negotiations with Austria, and it is alleged that she has virtually bribed Turkey to adopt the British standpoint with regard to the proposed international Conference.

SERVIAN CROWN PRINCE'S MISSION

Belgrade, 25 October – At the invitation of the Tsar the Crown Prince will leave here for Russia tomorrow (Monday). He will be the bearer of an autograph letter from King Peter.

Orders have been given by the War Minister for the immediate mobilisation of the whole of the first line of reserves.

Paris, 25 October – A telegram to the *Temps*, from Belgrade, announces that the Servian newspapers protest against the reported occupation by Austro-Hungarian troops of the Servian island of Bresina, in the River Drina.

It is stated that the Second Class Reserves will be called out shortly.

AUSTRIAN ATTACKS ON BRITAIN

Vienna, 24 October – The semi-official *Wiener Allgemeine Zeitung* this evening publishes the following account of the reasons for the sudden change in Turkey's foreign policy.

It says that the Young Turkish Party were in a difficult position, having no money to pay officials or army officers, and being unable to obtain credit abroad with which to buy munitions of war.

Great Britain suddenly came to their rescue, offering to give the Young Turkish régime its full financial and moral support, first furnishing a temporary loan of £5,000,000, and afterwards a consolidated loan of £50,000,000.

Great Britain also promised, in the event of a reactionary rising, to bring the warships now at Mitylene into the Dardanelles, provided that the Turkish Government consented to this course, and further, in the event of a war between Turkey and Bulgaria, to lend Turkey at least moral support – all this, however, being conditional upon Turkey first accepting the British standpoint regarding a European conference and breaking off direct negotiations with Austria.

The news of the breaking off of negotiations at Constantinople arouses much bitterness against Great Britain in Vienna, and the Press continues its attacks on that country.

TURKEY HURRYING UP RESERVES

Paris, 25 October – A correspondent of the *Action* telegraphs from Koniah that he has been travelling for two days on the completed section of the Koniah-Bagdad Railway in Turkish Asia Minor, and that everywhere he saw trains full of reserves.

The stations were encumbered with troops and munitions of war. The people believe that war is imminent, and display great enthusiasm.

The massacre of 4,000 Armenians at Dijar-Kedir, he says, is confirmed by eye-witnesses.

SERVIA AND MONTENEGRO ALLIED

Paris, 25 October – The *Journal*'s Sofia correspondent says: "The Ministers have tendered their collective resignation to the King. They consider that, after their recent categorical and bellicose statements, they cannot adopt a submissive attitude and assent to the payment of indemnities."

The Belgrade correspondent of the *Matin* states that at the grand banquet which was given in honour of General Vukotitch, the Montenegrin envoy, King Peter gave the toast of Prince Nicholas of Montenegro, and formally stated that an alliance had been concluded between Servia and Montenegro with a view to the national defence.

30 October **1908**

SERVIA'S PLAN

BOSNIA AND HERZEGOVINA SELF-GOVERNING UNDER A FOREIGN PRINCE

Paris, 29 October – It is semi-officially stated here that Servia, encouraged by Montenegro, anticipates that serious consequences will arise if the proposed Conference does not satisfy the aspirations of those States.

In Servian official quarters the desire appears to prevail that Bosnia and Herzegovina should be made autonomous under the authority of a foreign prince, and that the frontiers should be rectified in the direction of Herzegovina.

The *Temps* states that a preliminary agreement has been reached between Turkey and Bulgaria. Bulgaria proposes to pay an inclusive indemnity covering both the transfer of the Oriental Railway and the Eastern Rumelian tribute, though the expression "tribute" is not to be used, and negotiations are now proceeding to fix the amount of this indemnity.

2 November **1908**

SUPPORT FOR SERVIA

RUSSIA MAY REFUSE TO RECOGNISE ANNEXATION OF BOSNIA AND HERZEGOVINA

St Petersburg, 1 November – Public opinion is unanimous in considering that the chances of assembling a European Conference on the Balkan question are rapidly waning, and there are numerous signs which are regarded as indications that Russia will not accept the annexation of Bosnia and Herzegovina.

The Crown Prince of Servia and his brother Alexander lunched at Peterhof with the Tsar today.

The Press today is jubilant in the expectation that Russia will stand by the Slavs. The *Reich* remarks that so far as Russia is concerned the Servian cause is now safe.

4 November **1908**

BALKAN SITUATION GRAVE

DANGER OF WAR

There is an ominous movement of troops on each side of the frontier between Servia and Austria and never, since the Balkan

crisis was precipitated by Bulgaria's declaration of independence, has the danger of an outbreak of war been so great.

Austria has demanded the instant cessation of Servia's mobilisation, which she regards as aimed solely at herself. Servia meanwhile is feverishly pushing on her war preparations, and massing her troops around Belgrade, where 60 new quick-firing guns arrived yesterday.

It is proposed that the capital should be moved from Belgrade, which is, from its geographical position, peculiarly open to attack from Austria, to some town further from the frontier, and less accessible to the Austrian forces.

In Russia public opinion is veering round in favour of the Servians, who are assured of Russia's moral support, at least.

AUSTRIA THREATENS WAR

Belgrade, 2 November (midnight) – The Austrian Minister is reported to have given notice today that at the first cry of "Down with Austria" in Belgrade war would begin.

The Austrian 7th Army Corps is massed near the Servian frontier, threatening Belgrade, around which the Servian Army is disposed.

In military quarters there is the greatest activity. Ammunition is being hurried up and served out, and the commissariat arrangements are being perfected so as to allow the troops to take the field at a moment's notice.

Servian troops are marching east and west, for it is said that the Austrians are concentrating on Grotzka, on the Danube, 15 miles east of Belgrade, and also on the western frontier.

14 November **1908**

AUSTRIANS CONCENTRATING

ARMY OF 100,000 MEN WELL SUPPLIED WITH ARTILLERY ASSEMBLED IN BOSNIA

Belgrade, 13 November – It is reported here tonight that the Austrians are concentrating troops in Bosnia, where an army of 100,000 men, well supplied with artillery, has assembled.

Nine thousand infantry are said to be on the banks of the frontier river, the Drina. Belgrade Station is every night a scene of great activity, with the arrival of war materiel.

Aviation's infancy brought many unusual contraptions to the public's attention. Herbert Spencer is seen here at the controls of the Spencer Airship in the skies above Wandsworth during his attempt to fly around St Paul's Cathedral, 1908.

19 November **1908**

AUSTRIA AND MONTENEGRO

MOUNTAIN FORTIFIED AND PASS INTO HERZEGOVINA HELD BY 8,000 TROOPS

Cattaro (Dalmatia), 18 November – Consternation has been created here by the action of Montenegro in placing big guns on the summit of Mount Loveen. Some of the guns command the Bay of Cattaro, while others are directed against the town.

The situation is so threatening that the families of the military and civil officials have left the town and the town archives have been removed. Montenegro has placed guns in the lower slopes which dominate Cattaro, and has also had the Duga Pass, leading to Herzegovina, occupied by 8,000 troops.

28 November **1908**

ANOTHER CRISIS IN THE BALKANS

FRANCE'S REFUSAL TO MEDIATE BETWEEN AUSTRIA AND TURKEY

Relations between Austria-Hungary and Turkey have become very strained, the boycott of Austrian goods in Turkey causing great irritation in Vienna.

The boycott, of course, is as a result of the recent annexation by Austria of the Turkish provinces of Bosnia and Herzegovina. France has been approached by Austria to act as mediator but has refused.

The situation is regarded as distinctly dangerous. One result of it may be to hasten the formation of the proposed conference of Powers, in order to regulate the altered situation in the Balkans.

LITTLE HOPE OF SOLUTION

Constantinople, 27 November – The boycott of Austrian trade and shipping has undergone no change, notwithstanding the promise of the Porte to remedy it so far as the Customs House porters and lightermen are concerned.

Austro-Hungarian diplomatic circles, while waiting a few days longer before undertaking a fresh step, nevertheless appear to entertain little hope of a satisfactory solution, and consequently view the situation with concern.

As a matter of fact, public opinion is stronger than ever in favour of the maintenance of the boycott, thus rendering the task of the Government exceedingly difficult.

GERMANY'S OFFER

Paris, 27 November – The *Echo de Paris* declares that the relations between Turkey and Austria-Hungary have become very strained, and that Austria has taken steps which the Turks might regard as provocative. It is proposed to demand the intervention of France at Constantinople in order to smooth away difficulties.

A telegram from Constantinople to the same journal says: "Baron Marschall, the German Ambassador, on the occasion of his last interview with the Sultan, offered his Majesty the good offices of Germany in bringing about an arrangement between Austria-Hungary and Turkey on the subject of Bosnia-Herzegovina.

"In Germany it is also believed that the Government will use its influence in Austria in the direction of moderation."

FRANCE'S REFUSAL

Paris, 27 November – The French Government has refused the request of Austria to intervene in the dispute with Turkey. France, solicited by Baron von Aehrenthal, the Austro-Hungarian Foreign Minister, to use her good offices at Constantinople with the object of putting an end to the boycott of Austrian shipping and goods, relied that, notwithstanding her desire to facilitate the maintenance of peace, she was obliged to abstain from intervention in the matter.

It is understood on excellent authority that a defensive agreement between Servia and Turkey is on the point of being signed.

Montenegro will not be a contracting party to the agreement, but a promise will be made to her that in the event of an attack by Austria, Turkey will undertake her defence.

In view of the attitude of Italy, Austria, it is thought, will doubtless be obliged to come to terms or declare war under very disadvantageous conditions.

The Suffragette movement gathered pace in the early years of the 20th century as the activists campaigned for women's rights. Here, Mrs Emmeline Pankhurst, Mrs Drummond and Miss Christabel Pankhurst give themselves up at Clement Inn, London, Autumn 1908.

2 December **1908**

8,000 TROOPS FOR BOSNIA

RAILWAY TRAFFIC STOPPED TO FACILITATE PASSING OF AUSTRIAN TRANSPORT

Vienna, 1 December – A telegram from Budapest states that the Hungarian-Croatian Shipping Company has received orders to hold ships in readiness at Ragusa, Dalmatia, sufficient for the transport of 8,000 men. Traffic to Bosnia and Herzegovina, via Croatia and Dalmatia, it is added, has been stopped, all facilities being reserved for military purposes.

Belgrade, 1 December – The Turkish Government has permitted the transport of another consignment of war material for Servia through Turkish territory. This last consignment consists of six carloads of guns, 30 of ammunition and 12 of rifles.

Paris, 1 December – The Constantinople correspondent of the *New York Herald* (Paris edition) states that a Russo-Italian Convention relative to the Balkans, the nature of which is at present a secret, has received the supreme sanction of the two States.

57

Winston Churchill and Lloyd George (standing behind Churchill's left shoulder) were two of the most prominent politicians of the early 20th century.

Cafe

The Threat of War Passes

9 December **1908** – 29 March **1909**

Winston Churchill would become an influential figure in British politics after Herbert Asquith was installed as Prime Minister in 1908.

9 December **1908**

RUMOURS OF WAR

AUSTRIAN ARMY MOBILISED AND 150,000 TROOPS CONCENTRATED ON FRONTIERS

Paris, 8 December – A dispatch from Udine to the *Matin* says the Austrian Army is now entirely mobilised. A force of 150,000 men is drawn up on the frontiers of Servia and Montenegro, while 40,000 more are expected from Trieste.

The *Matin*, despite all the denials emanating from Austria, continues to publish numerous telegrams from its correspondents at Belgrade, Budapest and Udine, reporting the mobilisation and dispatch of troops into Bosnia, on the Montenegrin and Servian frontiers, and opposite the Sanjak of Novi-Bazar.

10 December **1908**

WILL AUSTRIA YIELD?

REPORTED OFFER OF £2,000,000 INDEMNITY TO TURKEY FOR ANNEXATIONS

Paris, 9 December – According to the latest advices from Constantinople negotiations have been reopened between Turkey and Austria, and Austria is stated to have offered Turkey an indemnity of £2,000,000 for the annexation of Bosnia and Herzegovina.

It is stated by the Paris *Petit Parisien* that Austria has now mobilised 200,000 men, and has been involved by the crisis in an expenditure of about £6,000,000.

AIRSHIP INVASION OF ENGLAND

GERMAN PREDICTS LANDING OF 100,000 MEN IN HALF AN HOUR

Berlin, 9 December – Government Councillor Rudolf Martin, whose name still figures on the list of officials of the Imperial Ministry for the Interior, although disciplinary proceedings against him will shortly come before the Supreme Court at Leipsic, this evening delivered a remarkable lecture to a crowded audience on the subject of Anglo-German relations, with special reference to the recent speech of Lord Roberts.

Herr Martin pointed out many indications of the existence of an uneasy feeling in England regarding the danger of attack by Germany, and asked the reason for the increased uneasiness, which is being felt just now.

AERIAL FLEET'S AID

The cause, he declared, was to be found in the solution to the problem of aerial navigation.

Now that Germany possesses motor airships England recognised that she might suffer severely from aerial attack, the invention of practical airships and flying machines having now rendered it impossible for England to emerge successfully from war with Germany. Continuing, Herr Martin declared that war between Germany and England would inevitably lead to the landing of a large German army in England.

During the war Germany would rapidly build a large aerial fleet, which, operating from Ostend or Calais, would effectively aid the German fleet in combating the British naval forces.

It was not the growth of the German fleet, but the invention of motor-airships, which, in case of war, would enable Germany to defeat England.

The fact that at the present time Germany only possesses a small number of motor-airships and flying machines did not affect the question.

TWO YEARS' WAR

War between England and Germany would last at least two years, and during this period Germany would be able to construct such a fleet of motor-airships and flying machines that she could not only destroy the British fleets in the Channel and the North Sea, but could also convey an army through the air to England.

Moreover, after the destruction of the British fleets a German army could also be landed in England in the ordinary way by sea transport. The brothers Wright's flying machine was a most important invention, and undoubtedly would soon be made adaptable for army transport purposes.

Germany could construct 50,000 flying machines for £50,000,000, and, starting from Calais, could land 100,000 men on the Kentish coast within half an hour.

It is a noteworthy fact that Herr Martin presupposes violation of Belgian neutrality or the conquest of Northern France in the case of war with England. Herr Martin concluded by declaring that no one in Germany desired war with England, and expressed the sincere hope that England and Germany will do their utmost to maintain friendly relations and agree to form a powerful alliance.

23 December **1908**

EUROPEAN CONFERENCE

Paris, 22 December – The *Journal* reproduces an interview with

Baron von Aehrenthal, published in the *Russkoye Slovo* of Moscow. The Austro-Hungarian Minister of Foreign Affairs is represented as having said that the pour-parlers entered upon by his country with Russia with a view to arriving at an agreement on the subject of a European conference was proceeding in the most conciliatory spirit.

Austria is persuaded, like Germany, Italy and Great Britain, that the Powers must go to the conference with a clearly defined programme.

The Minister then endeavoured to justify the military measures taken by Austria on the ground of necessity of putting an end to the provocative acts of Servia and Montenegro.

In conclusion, Baron von Aehrenthal declared that an overwhelming majority of the Slavs throughout the empire was in favour of the annexation of Bosnia and Herzegovina.

24 December **1908**

NO COMPENSATION FOR TURKEY

Vienna, 23 December – With reference to the suggestion that the improvement in the position of the negotiations between Austria-Hungary and Turkey was due to the fact that Austria-Hungary would take over part of the Turkish national debt, the semi-official *Wiener Allgemeine Zeitung* declares tonight that Austria-Hungary will not give Turkey pecuniary compensation of any kind for the annexation of Bosnia and Herzegovina.

9 January **1909**

▲ Colonel Samuel Cody walks alongside British Army aeroplane number one, as it is towed by horses of the Royal Artillery along to Farnborough Common for a test flight.

13 January **1909**

TURKEY ACCEPTS AUSTRIAN OFFER

SERVIA DISAPPOINTED

There is a distinct and welcome change for the better in the Balkan situation, and, so far as Austria and Turkey are concerned, all danger of armed conflict is at an end.

Turkey yesterday formally accepted the Austrian offer of £2,500,000 as compensation for her lost provinces, Bosnia and Herzegovina, annexed by Austria at the commencement of the Balkan crisis.

The one condition annexed to Austria's offer – more perhaps to save her dignity than because any doubt existed on the point – was that Turkey should prove her to title to the provinces, which at the time of the seizure were, though part of the Turkish Empire, virtually administered by Austria.

This settlement will bring to an end the Turkish boycott of Austrian goods, which proved so efficacious a weapon, and which drew repeated protests from Austria.

It began at Salonika on 11 October 1908 with the refusal of dock workers to unload Austrian ships; and then came in quick succession similar refusals at other ports, and the destruction of goods of Austrian origin. By Christmas, it was estimated Austrian merchants had suffered to the extent of about £2,000,000 by loss of trade.

FEZZES DISAPPEAR

So unusual was the boycott that almost in a single day the red fezzes, the ordinary Turkish headwear, disappeared from the streets of Constantinople and other large cities, the reason being that they were all of Austrian manufacture.

But, though this settlement will be welcomed by the Powers as tending to clear the troubled air, it will not be favourably received by certain of the Balkan States, and to Servia in particular it is most unwelcome, for her politicians have built much on the antagonism of Austria and Turkey.

And there are other reasons why Servia and Montenegro also will regard the settlement with disfavour, for it recognises the dominion of Austria over a population essentially Serv, and will tend to quicken the fears, already aroused, that they in turn may share the fate of Bosnia and Herzegovina. They, too, lie between Austria and the sea.

PORTE ACCEPTS OFFER

Constantinople, 12 January – The Grand Vizier has informed the Marquis Pallavieni, the Austro-Hungarian Ambassador, today that he accepts in the name of the Turkish Government the proposal of Austria-Hungary to pay the Porte an indemnity of £T2,500,000. The difficulty has therefore been overcome.

The Grand Vizier did unsuccessfully endeavour to induce Austria-Hungary to increase the amount by half a million, but the Ambassador declared that an increase was quite out of the question, and if the offer was rejected he would break off negotiations.

The other concessions by Austria-Hungary, which are already known, are upheld – namely the restitution and abandonment of Austrian rights in the Sanjak of Novi Bazar, an increase in the customs to 15 percent, the admission of certain monopolies, the suppression of post offices in places where there are no other foreign post offices should the Porte desire so, and the abrogation of certain old privileges over the Albanian Catholics.

The negotiations are thus practically at an end, and the various points of the understanding will be embodied in a Protocol. It is believed that an understanding with Bulgaria will now be facilitated.

FEELING IN SERVIA

Belgrade, 12 January – It is stated that the Government has received official information that Turkey is about to accept the offer of the Austro-Hungarian Government of £T2,500,000 as compensation for Turkey's rights in Bosnia and Herzegovina.

A meeting of the Cabinet under the presidency of the King is now being held. Political circles here are much disappointed at the news.

"Even should Turkey accept," the Belgrade *Politica* said before the news of Austria's terms was made known, "Servians will not permit their brethren to be sold. Austria-Hungary must exterminate all Servians before she can take over Bosnia definitively."

WAR PREPARATIONS COMPLETE

Vienna, 12 March – The *Zeit* learns form authoritative sources that the newly-armed Field Artillery will from today be placed upon a strict war footing.

The Government factories have been working to this end for several months, and Austria's preparations for war are now complete.

The Inspector-General of the Remount Department, Major-General Baseak, is leaving for England in order to purchase horses.

25 February **1909**

RUSSIAN WARNING

St Petersburg, 24 February – The reservists' papers in the St Petersburg district have been calling in for verification.

The *Novoe Vremya* today publishes a spirited reply to what it describes as the Austrian and German threats, declaring that the German Government is trying to order Russia to "hands up", while Austria is violating Servian interests.

"We and our ancestors," the journal continues, "have more than once had foreign conquerors on our soil, and the bones of several hundred thousand remain as the only testimony of their rash attempts to assail the integrity of Russian territory.

"We do not want to go to war with anyone, but we do not fear war, and even less will we be intimidated by empty phrases. If Austria and Germany attacked Russia they would not have to deal with her alone. Berlin and Vienna should reflect what would remain of the German and Austrian Empires after such a conflict.

"Not that we believe in war with Germany, Austria would find herself isolated, notwithstanding German assurances. Germany will not risk her own existence; she would prefer to secure for nothing the German portion of the remains of Austria after a war with Russia, rather than to stake all she has acquired by the work of generations."

AUSTRIA PREPARES

Paris, 24 February – The *Matin*'s Vienna correspondent states that activity prevails at the arsenals and among the general staff. During last week the troops on the frontier were reinforced by 20,000.

It is reported that General Etzendorf has drawn up a plan for the occupation of Servia. In military circles a Servian expedition is talked of carelessly – as an affair for the police – which will last only a few days.

12 March **1909**

BALKAN WAR CLOUD PASSES

BELGRADE WAR PARTY SAYS RUSSIA HAS ABANDONED SERVIA

With the definite abandonment yesterday by Servia of all claims for compensation from Austria-Hungary for the annexation of Bosnia and Herzegovina, the danger of war in the Balkans seems to have definitely passed away.

In reply to the presentations of Russia, which warned Servia against the danger of assuming a warlike attitude and insisting on compensation, Servia replied that she had no desire to cause war, claimed no compensation, and left the whole question of the annexation to the Powers.

This reply was embodied in a Circular Note telegraphed to the Servian Legations in the European capitals for communication to the respective governments, and this Note was yesterday presented at the Foreign Office in Vienna.

Less satisfaction is expressed in Vienna at Servia's Note than was expected, and a Servian boycott has been declared against Austrian steamers on the Danube and Sava rivers.

AUSTRIAN SHIPS TO BE BOYCOTTED

Belgrade, 11 March – The majority of the Servian papers are satisfied with the Circular Note, but impatiently await Austria's attitude.

The *Lista Politica*, the journal of the War Party, expresses its dissatisfaction in strong tones, declaring that Russia has abandoned Servia, and that the Serv nation is convinced that it must fight Austria to the death. In the Skupstina today, M Milovanoics, Minister for Foreign Affairs, made a statement upon the situation, and read the Russian Note and the Servian Circular. Although no objections were raised, his explanation was coldly received.

It is stated on good authority that the next Cabinet meeting will deal with the Austrian Note, and that the Servian Government will politely decline to enter into direct negotiations with Austria.

On the occasion of the opening of a steamship service on the Danube and Sava today a boycott was declared against Austrian vessels.

VIENNA CRITICAL

Vienna, 11 March – The contents of the Servian Circular Note appear to have given less satisfaction here than was anticipated. It is remarked that Servia's renunciation of her territorial claims is addressed to the Powers, and not to Austria-Hungary.

But, while the Note is not entirely satisfactory to official circles here, it is thought to some extent to encourage the hope that war will be avoided, as it offers a prospect of further negotiations, which promise, however, to be protracted and difficult.

CLAIMS ABANDONED

The following communiqué was issued yesterday by the Servian Government:

"The Servian Government, replying to the friendly advices of the Russian Government, pointed out that its position towards the Dual Monarchy after the annexation proclamation had remained normal, that Servia had no intention of causing war, nor desire to change the legal relations between the States, but was continuing to perform her obligations towards the Monarchy.

"Adhering, as she had always done, to the principle of reciprocity, Servia maintains that the annexation question is a European question, and, therefore, the final decision rests with the Powers. Relying upon the advice and justice of the Powers, Servia leaves her cause to them, and asks for no compensation whatsoever from the dual monarchy."

17 March **1909**

IS GREAT BRITAIN'S SUPREMACY SAFE?

GERMAN MENACE

There has been such an enormous development in Germany not only in the provision of shipyards and ships, but what is more important, in the provision of gun mountings, turrets and armament, that from a point of view of national security we can no longer take to ourselves the consoling reflection – as we did a year ago – that we have the advantage of speed in the rate at which ships can be built.

The remarkable debate in the Houses of Commons last night on the Naval Estimates of 35 millions for the year closed round Germany. And it was in answering Mr Balfour's attack on the Government programme that Mr Asquith made this admission.

"No matter what the cost, the safety of the country must be assured" was one of the almost bellicose phrases with which Mr McKenna, the keen, clean-shaven barrister who answers in the House of Commons for the Navy as First Lord of the Admiralty, introduced the Naval Estimates.

"The safety of the country stands above all other considerations," said Mr McKenna amid a roll of Unionist cheering, the Little Navy Party sitting glum and silent in the midst of the thronged Liberal benches.

The First Lord went over the shipbuilding programme for the year as set forth in the Navy Estimates. These include:

- Four Dreadnoughts to be laid down this year and completed within two years.
- Preparations for rapid construction of four more Dreadnoughts in April 1910.
- Six protected cruisers this year.
- Twenty destroyers.
- A number of Submarine boats for which £500,000 is allowed.
- Construction of an aerial vessel for experiment.
- New constrictions this year to cost £8,885,194.

During the recital the House sat silent and critical. The tremendous issues involved seemed to deeply impress the remarkable audience.

The Prince of Wales sat in the Peers' Gallery in the familiar seat of royalty over the clock. At his right hand were naval attachés of foreign Powers, watching with lynx eyes every expression of feeling in the British Parliament.

On the left of the Prince was a Peers' Gallery thronged with dukes, marquises, earls, viscounts and barons, immediately on the left of the Prince being Lord Cawdor, who was First Lord of the Admiralty in Mr Balfour's last Government. Every now and then the Prince of Wales, listening with deep, minute attention to every word of the debate, would turn to Lord Cawdor and a few words would pass between the two.

Mr Balfour, ex-Prime Minister and a great authority on national defence, rose as soon as the First Lord sat down. He tinged the debate with deep gravity.

We were faced with a novel position with regard to our sea power in comparison with other sea powers – different from anything seen for a century and a half, he said.

"For the first time there is bordering on the North Sea upon the waters that lave our own shores a great Naval Power, with capacity to compete with us in the construction of these great battleships… I say the naval programme, as presented by the Government, is utterly insufficient.

"What I am concerned about now is not how you get the money to build the necessary ships, but whether you build the necessary ships at all."

He dealt with the building of Dreadnoughts by England and Germany. "We have reached a point when it is a question, not whether we are obtaining the two-Power standard with regard to this particular class of ship, but whether we are obtaining a one-Power standard.

"I rejoice that we are on the friendliest terms with Germany. I do not suggest for an instant whether Germany is going beyond her legitimate interests.

"My question is whether, Germany having done what she has done and doing what she is doing, we are taking the only course which is consistent with the maintenance of our national safety."

Mr Balfour criticised the Government for having held back our shipbuilding programme to see whether other nations would do the same. He pointed to Mr McKenna's declaration, made earlier in the debate, that we had failed to get the other nations to do anything of the kind.

"Germany has used that time in making those enormous preparations upon plant, machinery and docks which have put

Germany in a position, compared with us, in which no nation up to the present time has ever been."

Mr Balfour went on to maintain by figures that through the Government keeping back the naval programme during the past two or three years, while Germany had gone forward with her shipbuilding, Germany would be completing the building of Dreadnoughts in the years 1910-11-12 to such an extent that the following would be the relative condition of affairs at the dates named:

	Britain	Germany
December 1910	10 Dreadnoughts	13 Dreadnoughts
July 1911	16 Dreadnoughts	17 Dreadnoughts

Mr Balfour asked the House not to delay in restoring this country to its proper ratio of naval supremacy.

The Prime Minister rose to the accompaniment of a loud burst of Liberal cheering as Mr Balfour sat down. The Prime Minister astonished the House by saying that the British Government had gone to Germany and asked her to join with us in retarding the increase of armaments, but Germany had declined to do so.

"There is no idea," said Mr Asquith in tones of deep gravity, "that our diplomatic relations with Germany are unsatisfactory now, or are likely to become so. In fact, recent events have tended to remove rather than erect possible barriers between Germany and ourselves. That it should continue is our hope and desire.

"But," said the Prime Minister, "Germany has informed us that her shipbuilding programme was not framed with respect to ours, but was governed by her own needs.

"If we built 100 Dreadnoughts," said the Prime Minister, "Germany would go on with her own programme. If we built no Dreadnoughts at all Germany would go on with her programme just the same. The Germans, like other nations, are the best judges of their own national requirements."

Mr Asquith then went on to quote other figures to show that, if we wished, we could, by November 1911, build 16 Dreadnoughts against Germany's 13.

In conclusion, Mr Asquith said the Government were most anxious to save money for the purpose of social reform, instead of having "this vast, horrible, devastating, sterilising expenditure," but it was a supreme paramount necessity.

Man of all parties listened mute, full of profound thought. Not for 20 years, writes our parliamentary correspondent, has the name of a "great friendly Power" been so freely mentioned by Ministers and ex-Ministers as the name of Germany last night.

THE LORDS AND AIRSHIPS

While the shadow of German Dreadnoughts on the sea loomed over the House of Commons the spectre of German aeroplanes of war rose in the House of Lords.

Lord Montagu of Beaulieu raised the question, pressing the Government as to what they were doing respecting air-warships. Germany and France, he said, had made great advances in the direction of practical dirigible balloons and aeroplanes.

Within a year or two foreign Powers, he believed, would have a considerable fleet of military balloons and airships capable of travelling 35 miles an hour and carrying six or eight men in each and explosives.

Lord Crewe, for the Government, announced that the Committee of Defence had given serious attention to the subject. The sum of £19,000 had been allocated for the Army for the war aeroplane and balloon purposes. France spent last year £47,000, Germany had allocated £133,751 and Austria £5,500.

These aeroplanes and war balloons might revolutionise the warfare of the future, said Lord Crewe, and the Government was watching developments.

DEMAND FOR INCREASE

The Prime Minister's speech last night not only carried conviction to the House generally, but it convinced many of those members who hitherto have supported the proposal to restrict any further increase in the Navy Estimates.

Immediately after Mr Asquith had spoken there was a hurried consultation in the Lobby of the Liberal members who were expected to support Mr Allan Baker's motion opposing any further increase in the Estimates.

Many of these members frankly announced that as a consequence of the Prime Minister's statement they would no longer oppose the Government's proposal, and it is highly improbable that the resolution will now be moved.

Among members of Parliament the gravest phase of the Prime Minister's utterance is admitted to be the frank refusal to apply the two-Power standard test to Dreadnoughts.

Mr Asquith pointed out that the comparison of the strength of Great Britain and Germany in capital ships was a different question altogether to that comprised in what was known as the two-Power standard.

The careful comparison that the right honourable gentlemen drew of the relative positions of the two fleets for the next three years was thought on both sides of the House not to permit a sufficient margin of safety, and there is no doubt that a strong

Under the personal supervision of the Kaiser a great German fleet of super Dreadnoughts was constructed, each ship an improvement on the British ships, so we were told.

demand will be made for an increase.

It may be taken for granted that the Government will have no difficulty in getting the vote they ask for, and in obtaining the power to anticipate provision for next year. Indeed, the advocates of a larger Estimate point to the speech of the Premier as confirming all their criticisms, and in the light of disclosures made in Parliament today there is no doubt that the Government could easily obtain all the money that they cared to ask for.

AUSTRIA PREPARING

The prevailing tone in Austria, following on the publication of Servia's reply to that Power on the Balkans question, is one of pessimism.

Reuter's Vienna correspondent learns that the Austro-Hungarian Government will reply to the Servian Note during the present week, stating that the Note is unsatisfactory, and demanding a full and clear explanation of Servia's intentions.

In order to give additional emphasis to Austria-Hungary's Note, 66 battalions, now upon a higher peace footing in Bosnia, will be raised to a war footing, which is equivalent to an addition of 40,000 men.

The Austrian Press has received strict injunctions not to publish any news concerning military movements. The Bourse was greatly depressed yesterday, and prices fell several points.

26 March **1909**

KAISER'S ROLE IN BALKANS

Paris, 25 March – The *Temps* tonight, in an interesting statement on the German Emperor's role in the Balkan troubles, explains Germany's close solidarity with Austria.

At the beginning of the Balkan crisis Germany hinted that she was prepared to act as the friend of both parties, but the proposals of the German Foreign Office were completely changed, owing to the personal action of the Emperor William.

For some time past, it appears, the relations between the Kaiser and the Archduke Francis Ferdinand, heir to the throne of Austria, had not been as cordial as they might have been. The Emperor saw in the Austro-Servian trouble a chance of placing himself definitely on good terms with the Archduke.

Thereupon he wrote to the Archduke Francis Ferdinand a warm personal letter, promising his full and unreserved support to Austria. This personal undertaking of the Kaiser completely bound German diplomacy to unreserved support of Austria, and explains Germany's present attitude.

29 March 1909

GERMANY'S IDEAL ENGLAND'S DANGER

CHILDREN OF FATHERLAND TAUGHT TO EXPECT WAR WITH US

by Mr Bart Kennedy

When I went to Germany in my professional capacity as correspondent I had no idea at all of writing as to the points of friction between Germany and England. In fact, I thought this kind of thing had been overdone, and my intention was to write sympathetically of this great people as I saw them.

But as soon as I got there I was fronted with overwhelming evidence to the effect that Germany intended to make war upon England as soon as the time was ripe. This evidence came absolutely from all sides.

Every Englishman I met was full of it. It was in the air; I heard it from ministers of the Gospel, as well as from laymen.

And not only did I hear it from Englishmen, I heard it from the Germans. The very students of Heidelberg were full of the idea. When I was watching the duelling on the floor of the Hirsch Gasse in Heidelberg I was told that it was a fine thing to develop the fighting instinct of the Germans so that they would come out well in their inevitable struggle with England.

I heard this talk of the German idea of war with England in the Reichstag. Socialist deputies themselves, when I put the thing straight to them, admitted that war was inevitable.

A well-known English clergyman in Germany's leading university town assured me that the very children in the schools were taught to expect war with us.

Fronted with this overwhelming evidence from everyone, even to the men of peace who belonged to the Salvation Army, I wrote my book, *The German Danger*, for I felt that I would not be doing my duty as an Englishman did I not endeavour to warn my country of the danger to its very existence.

This is nearly three years ago, and I was spoken of in the Radical Press as a mischievous and alarmist writer. But I am sorry to say that the development of the facts has more than given a reason for my warning at the time.

Germany absolutely means to make war upon us as soon as she is ready. There is no getting out of this. It is as plain as the sun at noonday. She has no real need for the fleet she is building. It is aimed directly at us. The ideal of a German statesman is to make and consolidate a vast German Empire, the basis of which shall be nearly the whole of Europe. They dream of subjecting Holland, and of merging Austria at the very least.

They dream of making France a subject State. They dream of breaking irrevocably the power of England. And who is the observer that shall say that they are not shaping towards the realising of this dream?

What is the use in talking? What is the use of being blind? Germany will kill us if she can.

And are we to wait while they are calmly and securely getting ready to dispute our mastership of the seas? We are to be fools and idiots.

Even the most optimistic assurances of the Government now in power give cause for the gravest alarm. The most optimistic assurance says that it will be from five to seven years before the Germans will have a chance to rival us in the struggle for the mastery of the seas.

And we must wait!

I am against war, as any thinking man must be. But we live in a world of war. We live in a world of facts.

If it were possible to come to an arrangement with Germany I would say let us do so. But this is absolutely impossible. Germany ignores our assurances and builds ship upon ship, while she throws peace-dust in the eyes of our Press. And we must wait!

But I say we must not wait. Our time is now. Germany intends to fight us, and it is not for us to await the moment favourable for our enemy. It is not the moment for polite words. It is the moment for deeds.

I am sorry to have to say this, but I fail to see why England should take even the slightest chance of being broken as a nation and scattered as a race. Why, even the very Kaiser himself has in effect admitted that the Germans intend to make war upon us!

No one denies the right that the Germans have to possess their ideal of world-supremacy. But we Englishmen are the blindest fools if we give them the slightest chance to realise their ideal.

Our time is to fight now – instantly. We don't want to fight; but we are forced. Even the present Government realises the dread gravity of the situation. They realise it, even when they are putting forth their most optimistic assurances. They realise that their country is in danger.

Germany cannot be world-supreme, as she wishes to be, unless she breaks us as a nation. And she is shaping her naval force to this end. And there are people in England who tell us we must wait.

But we must not wait. The slogan must go out now to all men of the British race. For now is the time for us to fight. Now is the time for us to grasp the nettle.

The German Menace

30 March **1909** – 25 September **1912**

As Great Britain ushered in a second new monarch in less than a decade after more than 60 years of stability, politicians began to suspect that it was not a Slavic nation that would endanger world peace, but Germany.

◀ Crowds line the street of London as the funeral cortège of King Edward VII passes by. The King had ruled for just nine years following the death of his mother, Queen Victoria, in 1901.

27 July **1909**

LONDON'S WELCOME TO HERO OF CHANNEL FLIGHT

M. BLERIOT ENTHUSIASTICALLY RECEIVED AT VICTORIA

LUNCH AT THE SAVOY

AEROPLANE EXHIBITED

Mr Haldane Pays Tribute to Courage of Monoplanist.

M. Louis Bleriot, the hero of the Channel flight, conquered London, yesterday.

The first man to cross by aerial machine the strip of water separating England from the rest of Europe visited the Metropolis for the purpose of receiving *The Daily Mail* prize of £1,000, and his welcome was wildly enthusiastic.

He was entertained to luncheon at the Savoy Hotel by Lord Northcliffe, who had invited a distinguished company to meet the famous aviator.

Today and tomorrow M. Bleriot's monoplane, on which he achieved his great flight, remains at Selfridge's, in Oxford Street, where all who wish may see it. Thousands of people inspected it yesterday.

Louis Bleriot in the cockpit of his monoplane with Mr Anzani, the designer and constructor of the engine, prior to his departure from Calais in 1909.

LONDON'S WARM WELCOME

London welcomed M. Bleriot, the winner of *The Daily Mail* £1,000 prize, with open arms yesterday. Long before the train bringing M. Bleriot and his happy wife from Dover was due at Victoria the station approaches were besieged with people anxious to get a view of the famous flier.

His train steamed in at 1.15, and the scene on the arrival platform was one long to be remembered.

Elaborate precautions had to be taken to secure M. Bleriot from the excessive enthusiasm of his admirers, and special barriers had to be formed.

A great cheer, and cries of "Bleriot!, Bleriot!, Bleriot!" arose when at last the train drew up and the hero of the hour stepped out. He still limped, as the result of his scalding accident some time ago.

Hobbling forward, he was presented to Lord Northcliffe, and then, leaning on his arm, and supported on the other side by

Louis Bleriot and his wife pose for a celebratory picture on the Dover cliffs.

Mr T. A. Snelling, a gentleman who, 37 years ago, cheered Captain Webb from the Admiralty Pier, Dover, on his successful swim across the Channel, he was escorted to a waiting motor-car.

Mme. Bleriot, a tall, handsome woman, who looked radiantly happy was presented with a lovely bouquet of pink carnations by Mme. Chereau, on behalf of the London house of Bleriot Limited.

A beautiful spray of lilies was also handed to Mme. Bleriot's famous husband by Lady Letchworth, who crossed from her carriage to do so because, she said, he is such a brave man.

LUNCHEON AT THE SAVOY

At the Savoy Hotel M. Bleriot, followed by crowds all the way from Victoria station, was entertained to luncheon by Lord Northcliffe on behalf of *The Daily Mail* for the purpose of receiving the prize offered by the proprietors for the first Channel flight.

In addition to Lord Northcliffe and M. and Mme. Bleriot, those present included Mr Haldane, War Minister; Sir Edward Ward, Permanent Secretary for War; Lieutenant E H Shackleton, Major Baden Powell, the French Ambassador (M Gambon), Sir Thomas Lipton, the Hon. Charles Rolls, Colonel Capper and M De Fieuriau (of the French Embassy).

At the reception Mr Haldane was the first to congratulate M. Bleriot, to whom he remarked that the flight across the Channel marked a great epoch in scientific history.

To cross the English Channel was one of those feats, he said, which marked the beginning of a new period. "You did it with wonderful ease" added Mr Haldane, "because you had great courage."

In the luncheon hall the French tricolour was hung from the walls and the ceiling, and the tables were covered with floral decorations embodying the national colours of the distinguished guests.

THE INITIATIVE OF FRANCE

Lord Northcliffe, in proposing the health of M. Bleriot, said the hurried honour of the occasion was due to the quickness of a man whom the whole world now knew truly represented the old blood of Gaul.

Referring to the pleasure which it gave to England to signal the triumph of M. Bleriot, Lord Northcliffe said that in his opinion the peace of the world depended upon the present cordial understanding between the two countries.

The speaker also paid a tribute to the work of Lieutenant Shackleton, who was seated next to the inventor, and said that the two men had done more for modern civilisation than any other two men in the world.

Then, speaking in French, Lord Northcliffe said: "I wish to say in their own language to M. and Mme. Bleriot how deeply we, all of us, rejoice to see that the initiative of la Belle France, who has already given us so many inventions – balloons, photography, bicycles – to whom we also owe ironclads, the great development of the motor-car industry, colour photography, the marvellous discovery of radium – is now continued by the admirable undertaking of our guest of today.

"I wish also, through his Excellency M Gambon, to congratulate that noble country in having a son endowed with such parts and courage."

M. Bleriot, radiant and smiling, and wearing the ribbon of the Legion of Honour, had to stand for several minutes before he could find his voice, owing to the deafening cheers which greeted the toast.

AVIATORS MODEST REPLY

"I am deeply touched," he said, "by your welcome, a welcome which is altogether out of proportion to the feat which I have accomplished.

"I hope that France and England, already united by water – by the Channel that was below me during my flight – they now be still closer united by air.

"I drink to England and to her King."

Lord Northcliffe then presented M. Bleriot with a silver rose bowl, on behalf of the English directors of M. Bleriot's Lyndon Company, and the silver cup and £1,000 prize money awarded by *The Daily Mail*. He also announced that the Aero Club had decided to present M. Bleriot with the special gold medal of the society.

Mme. Bleriot was then presented with a bouquet on behalf of the Women's Aerial League of Great Britain.

HERO WORSHIP AT DOVER

A rousing send-off was given to M. Bleriot and his wife this morning when they left Dover for London at half-past nine.

The Mayor and Corporation of Dover received the aviator at the Lord Warden Hotel. There were few speeches, but much cheering.

No sooner had M. Bleriot left the hotel for the station than he learnt the cost of being famous.

He was besieged by autograph-hunters, men, women, and children holding out photographs, begging him for his autograph. The pencil he used for writing his name was worn down to a stump. As he stepped towards the reserved saloon of the train several well-dressed ladies pressed forward towards him and made as if to kiss him.

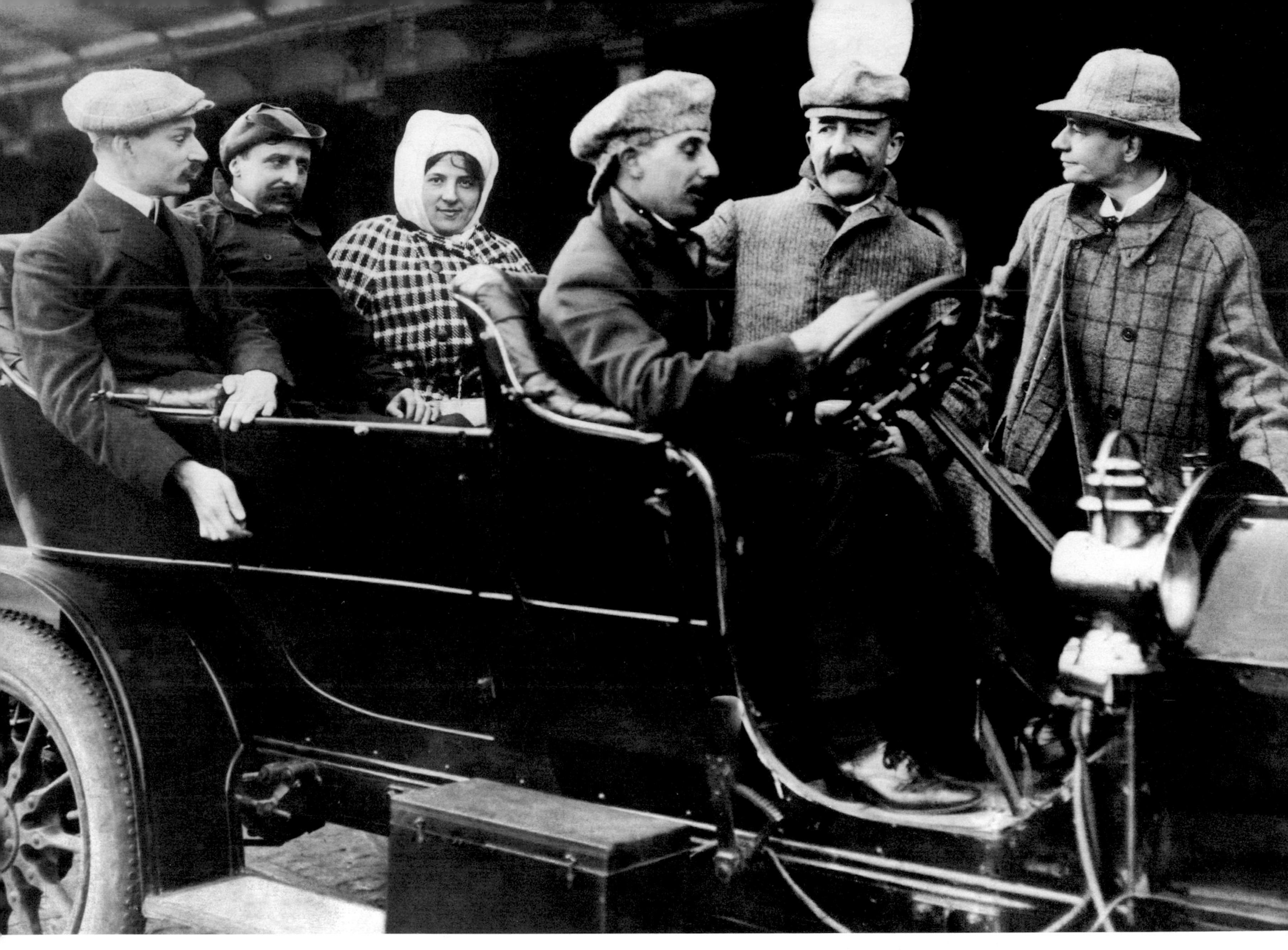

"You brave man" cried one lady, impetuously. The aviator hopped along on his sound leg as fast as he could, and looked somewhat relieved when safely inside the saloon.

When the train left Mme. Bleriot appeared much interested in the photograph of herself in *The Daily Mirror*.

The Bleriot monoplane, when it left here at an early hour this morning, was packed on two open railway trucks and consigned as flying machine damaged.

MONOPLANE VIEWED BY PUBLIC

All day long people gazed yesterday at the monoplane in which M. Louis Bleriot accomplished his marvellous flight.

In the early hours of the morning it arrived at Cannon Street station, and thence was conveyed to Selfridge's Stores, Oxford Street, where it remains on view to the public free of charge today and tomorrow.

Mr H Gordon Selfridge, in consideration of this arrangement, is giving £200 to the London Hospital, and during the time it is exhibited the aeroplane is insured for £1,000 against fire, theft, or accident.

French aviator Louis Bleriot leaves Dover Quay for breakfast at the Lord Warden Hotel following his historic flight across the English Channel.

The Daily Mirror

THE MORNING JOURNAL WITH THE SECOND LARGEST NET SALE.

No. 1,793. | Registered at the G. P. O. as a Newspaper. | TUESDAY, JULY 27, 1909. | One Halfpenny.

LONDON'S WELCOME TO M. BLERIOT: CHEERING THE INTREPID AVIATOR AS HE LEAVES VICTORIA.

M. Louis Blériot, the aviator, who wrote a new page of history on Sunday, arrived in London yesterday to receive the £1,000 prize offered by *The Daily Mail* to the first man to cross the English Channel in a machine heavier than air. Some time before the train was timed to arrive at Victoria crowds flocked into the station and the yard outside, and as the intrepid aviator stepped from the train he was greeted with a roar of welcome. The picture shows M. Blériot (who is raising his hat in acknowledgment of the cheers) leaving Victoria in a motor-car for the Savoy Hotel, where he was entertained to luncheon.

5 January **1910**

"BLATCHFORDIAN SOCIALIST" MR HENRY K JONES WARNS OF THE GERMAN MENACE

None of the election speakers on the Unionist side is more interesting than Mr H K Jones, a Socialist, who, because long residence in Germany has convinced him of the truth of Mr Robert Blatchford's articles on "The German Menace", has come out as a strong supporter of Lord Charles Beresford's candidature. He is pictured talking outside the dockyard gates at Portsmouth yesterday . . .

MR BALFOUR ON THE NAVY AND TARIFF REFORM

EX-PREMIER ON NAVAL POSITION

Mr Balfour, the Unionist leader, opened his political tour of the provinces last night at Hanley with a solemn warning on the moral danger into which the Liberal Government had plunged the country. Never had the ideals of the two parties in the State been so widely divergent, said Mr Balfour.

He would not now deal with the fundamental liberty of every parent to choose the kind of religious teaching which the child ought to have, nor should he touch on the subject which was near to his heart – those improvements in the land system which might increase the number of those directly interested as owners of the soil.

He would confine himself to the subjects of the Navy, Socialism and tariff reform.

They were charged with using the Navy for party purposes, but the Opposition had in fact refrained from bringing in any question in the House which might injure the position of this country.

Not until they were driven to it did they raise the question of the adequacy of our naval preparations and the relative strength of the fighting ships of the first class.

And when they raised it he ventured to say that there could not be found more conclusive justification of the course which they pursued than the speeches made by some members of the Government.

When the Unionist Party left office they left the present Government with an ample supply of battleships and naval stores. Where did they stand now? (A voice: "Upside down.")

They stood upside down – a position which for the very best acrobat was one of very unstable equilibrium.

"INCOMPARABLY WEAKER"

"During the earlier years," continued the ex-Premier, "they were occupied in amiable philanthropic but perfectly futile and fruitless negotiations with regard to the limitation of armaments.

"While they were talking, other nations more alert were not only adding to their armaments at a perfectly unprecedented rate, but were adding to their power of turning out ships.

"As regards the newest kinds of ships, the actual fighting strength, our position is incomparably weaker, and nobody can deny it.

"Nobody can say as compared with other nations in 1909–10 – I fear still less in 1911, and possibly still less in 1912 – that our strength is comparable to the position in actual ships when we resigned four years ago.

"When we left office it was in our power to modify our naval estimates each year by what we saw foreign nations were doing, because we could build ships faster than any other nation. That is all altered.

"I do not say the Government are to blame for the alteration, but they are to blame for having kept back from the House of Commons and the country, long after they knew it themselves, that this vital and fundamental alteration had taken place."

EMPIRE ON SUFFERANCE

"They knew it; they told us nothing about it; they took no steps to remedy it; and it was not until the matter leaked out or was extracted almost by a process of torture, that the country began to realise that we are now in a position which we have not been within the memory of living men – that our naval superiority in our own seas is threatened within the near future.

"We exist as an Empire only on sufferance unless our Navy be supreme, and I for one am not content to exist on sufferance."

Statesmen and diplomats abroad, continued Mr Balfour, had come to the conclusion – he believed utterly wrongly – that we were not alive to the sense of our responsibilities, and that we were predestined to succumb in some great contest to a country which did face facts.

"Now, I believe that all these prophets will find themselves mistaken. But while I give the note of warning of our foreign critics let me say what is more to the point to my own friends here.

"Unless they bestir themselves Great Britain will be in a position of peril which it has not known in the memory of their fathers, their grandfathers, their great-grandfathers.

The. Daily. Mirror

THE MORNING JOURNAL WITH THE SECOND LARGEST NET SALE.

No. 1932. Registered at the G. P. O. as a Newspaper. WEDNESDAY, JANUARY 5, 1910. One Halfpenny.

MR. HENRY K. JONES, A "BLATCHFORDIAN SOCIALIST," SUPPORTS LORD CHARLES BERESFORD AT PORTSMOUTH BECAUSE OF THE GERMAN MENACE.

None of the election speakers on the Unionist side is more interesting than Mr. H. K. Jones, a Socialist, who, because long residence in Germany has convinced him of the truth of Mr. Robert Blatchford's articles on "The German Menace," has come out as a strong supporter of Lord Charles Beresford's candidature. Above, he is seen talking outside the dockyard gates at Portsmouth yesterday. (1) "That man is no patriot!" (2) Heckled by a lady. (3) "If I have joked, don't think I do not see the gravity of the situation!" (4) "I have lived in Germany, and I know." (5) "The enemy are at your gates." (6) Listening to a question. (7) "As a Socialist, I don't want to see German plutocracy replace what I am trying to get rid of here." —(*Daily Mirror* photographs.)

"And if that position of peril should issue in some great catastrophe – which Heaven forbid! – it is a catastrophe once it has occurred from which this country will not again easily rise.

"I don't believe there is going to be war between this country and any great foreign Power. Heaven knows I don't desire it, and I don't believe it.

"But, please remember, the absolutely only way in which you can secure the peace which you all desire is that you shall be sure of victory if war takes place."

OTHER SPEAKERS

Lord Charles Beresford, at Portsmouth: "For construction alone Germany was this year spending £10,700,000, against our £10,200,000. For the first time in the history of the British Empire the Government of the day had voted less for construction than one single foreign Power."

13 January **1910**

FIVE CRUISERS, SIX DESTROYERS

FIRST PART OF CANADA'S NAVY, WHICH WILL BE AT SERVICE OF BRITAIN IN WAR

In the Dominion House of Commons, Ottawa, Sir Wilfred Laurier, the Prime Minister, introducing the Naval Defence Bill, said the Government were proceeding to organise a naval service on the lines of the Militia Act of Canada, including a permanent force, a reserve force, and a volunteer force. They would commence with the early construction of two cruisers of the Bristol class, three of the Boadicea class, and six destroyers of the improved Rover class.

An important provision in the Bill is that, in case of emergency, the Government may by an Order in Council place the fleet at the disposal of His Majesty for general service with the Royal Navy. Asked whether emergency meant war in Canada or abroad, Sir W Laurier replied: "War anywhere. If Great Britain is at war then Canada is liable to invasion and Canada is at war."

Mr Borden, leader of the Opposition, regarded the possibility of war with Germany as very real.

29 January **1910**

RECIPROCITY AND PEACE

"The exchange of commodities between Germany and England forms the basis of their commercial balance sheets, and the more the interchange of products increases the more both countries are enriched," said the German Ambassador last night at a dinner of German societies in London. The Germans, he added, had no intention of competing for supremacy on the sea.

5 February **1910**

POWERS AND CRETE

GENERAL RESOLVE TO OBTAIN PEACEFUL SOLUTION OF TURCO-GREEK CRISIS

The forthcoming visit of Baron von Aehrenthal, the Austrian Minister of Foreign Affairs, to Baron von Bethmann-Hollweg, the German Imperial Chancellor, at Berlin, is regarded as not being unconnected with the situation in the Near East.

The *Matin* learns on good authority from St Petersburg that Baron von Aehrenthal has promised Mr Isvolsky, the Russian Foreign Minister, to address a declaration to the European Powers advising them to maintain the status quo in the Balkans.

This policy of disinterestedness, it is added, will guarantee the peaceful evolution of Turkey and the Balkans, and thereby secure the peace of Europe for many years.

The Russian Press declares that war in the Near East can only be averted by the firmest action on the part of the protecting Powers. Cretan delegates cannot be permitted to attend the Greek National Assembly.

The renewal of troubles in Crete is preferable, the papers declare, to Turco-Greek hostilities and the risk of international complications.

12 February **1910**

GERMAN TURBINE TORPEDO-BOAT TRAVELS AT 36.3 KNOTS AN HOUR

GREAT SPEED ATTAINED BY THE *S166*, ONE OF THE NEW FLOTILLA OF 11 VESSELS

Germany's first complete flotilla of turbine torpedo-boats, consisting of 11 vessels of the newest type, is now in commission.

One of the vessels, the *S166*, maintained for a considerable period a speed of 36.3 knots, with an average on all her runs of 35.03 knots.

The highest speed previously attained by a German torpedo-boat was 34.72 knots, attributed to the *G171* during her trials last November.

25 February **1910**

GERMAN TROOPS ON THE CONGO

The *Tribune Congolaise* says that great excitement prevails in the Rusizi Kivu region on the Belgian side of the disputed frontier between the Congo and German East Africa in consequence of the concentration of German troops on the border.

26 February **1910**

HALF OF *ZEPPELIN III*, WHICH HAS BEEN CUT IN TWO FOR RECONSTRUCTION

The framework of the giant airship, *Zeppelin III*, has been cut in two, in order that the parts may be taken into the workshops for reconstruction. She is considered the fastest of the German military airships, having covered 60 miles in an hour.

28 February **1910**

TRIPLE ALLIANCE

GERMANY, AUSTRIA AND ITALY RENEW AGREEMENT FOR FURTHER 10 YEARS

According to a telegram from Milan, the *Corriere Della Sera* says that, as a result of the understanding arrived at between Count Aehrenthal and the German Chancellor, Herr von Bethmann-Hollweg, the Triple Alliance will be renewed for 10 years without modification.

This renewal of the Triple Alliance between Germany, Austria-Hungary and Italy is the outcome of the visit to Berlin of Count von Aehrenthal, the Austrian Foreign Minister.

"The Russians shall not have Constantinople" is one of the fundamental ideas of the Triple Alliance.

3 March **1910**

NAVY DEBATE IN THE COMMONS

Lord Charles Beresford raised the question of construction. He asked for an assurance as to our capability to turn out destroyers as quickly as Germany could.

"Germany averaged eight or nine months to build a destroyer. We averaged 19 months. Directly money was voted for shipbuilding in Germany that country immediately started to build.

"We have got an extraordinary system of putting down the money and beginning to build next year.

"Some of the 20 destroyers of the present year's programme have not been laid down yet," he declared.

CONTINGENT DREADNOUGHTS

In a speech earlier in the debate Mr McKenna announced that the four contingent ships would be ready in March 1912. Three of the four will be battleships and the fourth a huge armoured cruiser with a speed of about 30 knots.

The First Lord also mentioned that the Admiralty now estimated the time for the construction of a Dreadnought at 28 months. This included all the preliminary preparations. The time occupied from

HMS *Dreadnought*, the 18,110-ton battleship built at Portsmouth Dockyard, revolutionised naval power.

laying the keel would be 23 or 24 months.

HMS *Dreadnought*, an 18,110-ton battleship built at Portsmouth Dockyard, was a battleship of the British Royal Navy that revolutionised naval power. Her entry into service in 1906 represented such a marked advance in naval technology that her name came to be associated with an entire generation of battleships, known as the "Dreadnoughts". During the First World War, HMS *Dreadnought* served with the 4th Battle Squadron in the North Sea.

SIX DREADNOUGHTS

£40,000,000 REQUIRED FOR THE NAVY DURING THE COMING YEAR

One of the principal events in Parliament this week will be the presentation of the Navy estimates for 1910–11. As forecasted in the King's Speech, the estimates will show a "substantial increase", owing mainly, of course, to the unprecedented activity in the German naval shipbuilding yards and, naturally, the precise amount of this increase is being eagerly awaited.

This year £36,000,000, in rough figures, has been devoted to the British Navy, including the four contingent Dreadnought ships just ordered. The total amount for the coming year is expected to reach the high figure of £40,000,000.

What the Government's shipbuilding programme is remains a closely-guarded secret, but the general feeling among Unionists is that it ought to provide for the completion of at least six additional Dreadnought battleships by the spring of 1913, as well as several cruisers, destroyers and submarines.

29 March **1910**

GERMAN AEROPLANE SCHOOL

KAISER'S ORDER TO ARMY OFFICERS TO LEARN THE ART OF FLIGHT

The Kaiser, convinced that the aeroplane is destined to become an effective engine of war, has ordered that as many German Army officers shall learn to fly.

Captain Engelhardt, Orville Wright's pupil, will accordingly begin to instruct a number of German officers in the art of aeroplaning, and they, in turn, will teach their comrades in other regiments.

It is expected that in the near future a company of aviators will be attached to every regiment.

1 April **1910**

GERMANY'S NORTH SEA FLEET

For the first time in her history Germany will today have a fleet permanently stationed in the North Sea. Hitherto Kiel has been the principal headquarters of the Imperial Navy. But to have the fleet in the Baltic no longer agrees with the ideas of naval Germany, so the stronger and more modern divisions of the active battle fleet is today to be shifted into the North Sea and based at Wilhelmshaven.

The squadron is commanded by Vice-Admiral Pohl and consists of eight battleships, two armoured cruisers and three protected cruisers. Two of the battleships – the *Nassau* and the *Westfalen* – are super-Dreadnoughts of 18,500 tons, armed with 12 11-inch and 12 5.9-inch guns. The other battle units will be replaced by Dreadnoughts as soon as the new ships are delivered.

8 April **1910**

BRITAIN'S REPLY

ARMADA OF 120 SHIPS TO MUSTER IN NORTH SEA

An enormous British armada will assemble in the North Sea on 19 April when Admiral Sir William May, Commander-in-Chief of the Home Fleet, will have under his orders for a special combined cruise three complete and fully-equipped fleets. This great naval force will consist of the First and Second Divisions of the Home Fleet and also the Atlantic Fleet, a semi-independent command whose chief is Vice-Admiral Prince Louis of Battenberg.

The amassing of this great force – which includes 10 Dreadnoughts – in the North Sea is regarded as the Admiralty's answer to the transference of the German high-sea fleet from Kiel to Wilhelmshaven.

14 April **1910**

GERMANY'S AIR POWER

It is rather a startling situation when we find that Germany is mistress of the air in the same way we claim to be mistress of the seas. Thus Lord Montagu of Beaulieu explained in the House

of Lords last night. According to this distinguished expert the dirigibles possessed by the leading European nations in 1911 will be as follows:

- ⋆ Germany 94
- ⋆ France 40
- ⋆ Austria 6 or 7
- ⋆ Russia 6
- ⋆ England 5

Lord Lucas, the young Under-Secretary for War, reminded their Lordships that aviation was very much in its infancy. We and all other nations were simply experimenting.

There is being constructed for the Navy a large rigid dirigible, and it is possible another will be available during the next 12 months.

The Army has one non-rigid dirigible, and a new one is under consideration. Two foreign dirigibles are coming over, and if suitable they will be taken over by the War Office.

"The Government," added Lord Lucas, "are spending in the coming year on airship construction and experiments £100,000."

23 April **1910**

SECRET AGREEMENT

NAVAL WRITER ALLEGES AUSTRIAN-GERMAN PACT REGARDING DREADNOUGHTS

A secret agreement between the Austrian and German governments in regard to Austria's Dreadnought programme is declared by the naval correspondent of the *Globe* to have been arrived at. He quotes "an exceedingly high foreign diplomatic source" as his authority for stating that, should the Austrian Parliament refuse to vote the necessary funds, the German Government will purchase the four Austrian Dreadnoughts outright.

Work on two of the four has been begun, it is stated, without waiting for the sanction of Parliament.

◆ King George, Kaiser Wilhelm II of Germany and the Duke of Connaught at the funeral of King Edward VII, 20 May 1910.

◆ A V Roe, one of the early pioneers of British aviation, test flies the second Roe 1 Triplane at Wembley Park, Spring 1910.

24 June **1910**

BRITISH ARMY'S FLYING CORPS

WAR OFFICE SCHEME TO UTILISE SERVICES OF ENGLISH AIRMEN

A great scheme of national importance and interest is being formulated by the War Office for the complete and efficient defence of the country. Briefly, the scheme is to establish a special corps of British airmen, consisting of the most expert flyers in the country, who will act in an advisory and consultative capacity on all subjects relating to war in the air.

These gentlemen will, it is believed, be given commissioned rank on enrolment, and in the event of war their services will be absolutely at the disposal of the Government.

In peace time it will be their duty to meet and discuss the various intricate problems relating to war in the air, to give the War Office authorities the benefit of their valuable advice founded on actual

11

experiences and to devise the best types of flying machines and airships for all the purposes of war, scouting, defence and attack, and, in short, to help in securing for Great Britain, in conjunction with the able officers of the Aerial Department of the War Office, the efficient and permanent command of the air.

Such is the general idea of the scheme now contemplated, and it will certainly be received with the warmest and most enthusiastic approval of British airmen.

Mr Perrin, secretary of the Royal Aero Club, admitted that he had heard of the scheme. "I do not know," he said, "whether the new corps will be formed on the lines of the Army Motor Reserve, but the scheme will certainly be of real practical value. Already there are 20 Englishmen who have been awarded pilot certificates, and the number will be increased very considerably as our knowledge of the science of aerial aviation advances."

Up to the present both the War Office and the Admiralty have devoted their attention in aerial questions to the construction of dirigible balloons, but in future flying machines will also be built, and sheds for their accommodation are to be erected on Salisbury Plain and other parts of the country.

The mammoth dirigible balloon now in course of construction at Barrow is the first to be built for the Navy, and if it successfully fulfills the mission for which it is designed – namely scouting over sea for several days on end, without returning to its shed – a whole fleet of a similar type of vessel will be ordered.

It is also likely that the Army authorities will give orders for the construction of more ships of the type which recently made such a remarkably good midnight voyage from Aldershot to London and back.

It is recognised, however, that flying machines, as distinct from dirigible balloons, must inevitably play an important part in the next war, and hence the resolve to form a special corps of airmen, whose practical knowledge will prove of inestimable value to the country.

Naval and military officers have for a long time past been carrying out exhaustive private trials at their own expense of various types of flying machines, and it is known that they have made considerable progress towards overcoming the many difficulties associated with the art of airmanship.

It is obvious, of course, that these private and patriotic endeavours must be backed up by a wider national sentiment, and when the next Estimates are produced it will be found that a very much larger sum of money than the £100,000 at present allotted will be set aside for the airships and flying machines of both services.

American pioneer Samuel Cody leaving Brooklands in 1911. He was the first man to be killed in an air accident.

British aviation pioneer Claude Grahame-White, accompanied by a lady passenger, in his Henri Farman biplane.

5 September 1910

GUNPROOF WARSHIP

MOTOR-DRIVEN "CRUISER DESTROYERS" SAID TO BE CONTEMPLATED – 16.7-INCH GUNS

The *Vorwaeris* professes to have learned from a well-informed source that the British and German Admiralties are both working with feverish haste on a new model of an armoured monitor intended for use against Dreadnought cruisers which, while itself practically invulnerable, will be an irresistible opponent for vessels of the most powerful types.

The new Dreadnought destroyer is rendered possible by the substitution of motor internal combustion engines for steam, and her armament will be two 16.7-inch guns, throwing a projectile weighting 5,940lb.

There will be one turret amidships turning in all directions, and the vessel will be driven by four motors, each of 6,000hp, with a normal speed of 19 knots.

Her deck turret and free board will be so extraordinarily heavily armoured that the designers anticipate, while her almost three-ton projectiles will penetrate the armour of any Dreadnought, the low free board and heavy armour of the new vessel will be practically proof against 12-inch guns.

It is added that she will cost considerably less than the Dreadnoughts. The name to be given to the vessel is "cruiser destroyer".

If the report of the *Vorwaeris* (which is a Labour newspaper) proves true, the new model ship will mark a distinct advance in naval architecture, for she will be the first big warship to be driven by internal combustion engines.

The biggest naval guns known are the 13.5-inch, which are to be carried by the new British Dreadnought *Orion*, though Germany was credited with having experimented with a 14-inch weapon. The English 12-in guns – such as carried by the existing Dreadnoughts – throw a projectile of only 850lb, and the 13.5 a projectile of 1,250lb.

GERMAN GIBRALTAR

HELIGOLAND FORTIFIED AS A NAVAL BASE – HARBOUR EXTENSIONS

Germany's naval activities in the North Sea, upon which so much prominence has been thrown by the arrest of two Englishmen, Messrs Brandon and Trench, on a charge of espionage at Borkum, one of the German Frisian Isles, become very evident to a visitor at Heligoland.

This charming little island, formerly British, is far on the way to becoming Germany's Gibraltar. Already it is strongly fortified and garrisoned, and the great harbour extensions now in progress will enormously increase its naval value.

The red cliffs of the island not only add to the picturesqueness which makes it second only to Norderney among Germany's seaside resorts, but also make it easily defensible and hard to attack.

Steamers of the North German Lloyd and the Hamburg-America Companies serve Heligoland daily, many of them going on to Norderney. Teutons who affect maritime life always choose the route via Heligoland to Norderney, and the scenes on board are often harrowing.

Messrs Brandon and Trench allegedly first drew suspicion upon themselves by thinking all the seven Frisian Islands from Wangerooge to Borkum worth touring, after visiting Heligoland. This seemed all the more strange, except Wangerooge and Borkum, where alfresco picnics in bathing suits are popular, the islands have little interest to the tourist. All of them are flat and monotonous, and there are hardly any trees upon them.

Heligoland, however, is different, and would be popular with the English if more accessible. After it was ceded by Lord Salisbury to Germany, it was allowed to retain many privileges, notably the free importation of tobacco and cigars.

Hence there are special cabins on all steamers leaving here for German ports for a superlatively vigorous examination of baggage.

There is, of course, forbidden ground here, upon which only idiots or spies would trespass, but otherwise the island is singularly free from restrictions.

A visit to Heligoland is fast becoming a thing that all patriotic Germans with naval aspirations must undertake; indeed, they seem positively to enjoy the seasickness attendant on a voyage to Heligoland, regarding it as an essential factor of naval education.

28 September 1910

LORD C BERESFORD WARNS PREMIER

NEED OF MAKING IMMEDIATE PREPARATION FOR 1913–14

Lord Charles Beresford has addressed a remarkable "open letter" on the Navy to the Prime Minister. During the next few weeks, he says, there must occur a momentous crisis in the affairs of the nation and the Empire.

"If the right measures are taken by the executive Government the defences of the Empire may be secured. But if, in the contrary, the present opportunity be neglected, I will venture to affirm with such assurance as 50 years of public service may lend my words, that the position of the affairs with regard to the naval defence of the Empire will three years hence be fraught with a danger whose gravity I believe it to be difficult to exaggerate."

Lord Charles selects the year 1913–14 as the critical moment, because if the country is to be fully equal to the contingencies, which will then arise, due preparations must be begun immediately.

These preparations must be begun during the present autumn because, should they be postponed, the shipbuilding capacity of the country will prove unequal to the requirements of the case, which involve the completion of a large number of vessels by a definite date.

In order that the naval power of Great Britain may be maintained in its proper relation to the strength of the naval power of foreign nations three years hence, Lord Charles believes it to be absolutely essential that, in addition to the five capital ships which are to be laid down next year, seven more first-class armoured ships should be laid down . . .

"It is clear that three years hence our superiority over Germany will be reduced to four ships of the Dreadnought type. We shall be exactly equal to Germany and Austria combined; and inferior by four vessels to the Triple Alliance."

DREADNOUGHTS' 28 BIG GUNS

"WE KNOW WHAT IS OUR OBJECT," SAYS GERMAN VICE-ADMIRAL

The Wilhelmshaven correspondent of the *New York Herald* has been permitted to inspect the first squadron of the German High Sea Fleet, composed exclusively of four new Dreadnoughts which, he says, are masterpieces of design.

Next year the squadron is to be reinforced by three more Dreadnoughts that will have six big guns to fire ahead, six astern and eight on either broadside.

Vice-Admiral Pohl, in command of the squadron, remarked to the correspondent: "The development of the German Navy is in consonance with the genius of the German people. We know what is our object, and go steadily forward for its attainment."

15 October **1910**

GERMAN'S VIEW OF BRITISH ARMY

COLONEL WHO SAW MANOEUVRES SAYS IT IS NOT FIT TO FIGHT CONTINENTAL TROOPS

Colonel Gaedke, who attended the British Army manoeuvres in September, writing in the *Berliner Tageblatt*, expresses the conviction that if the British Army be compared with the French, German, Austrian or Japanese armies, the verdict can only be that, as at present constituted, it is not fit for conflict with a Continental army.

As a land power, Colonel Gaedke declares Great Britain has no place among the first-class military Powers. Nevertheless, the soldier material and the raw material in the form of officers are really eminently good and need yield to no others in the world.

13 February **1911**

AEROPLANE USED IN WAR

AIRMAN RUNS RISK OF BEING FIRED AT WHEN SCOUTING OVER MEXICAN DEFENCES

For the first time in the history of warfare an aeroplane has been successfully employed in the important work of reconnaissance. A Reuter message from New York reports a telegram from El Paso (Texas) stating that, despite warnings issued by the Mexican authorities that any airman who crossed the frontier would be fired upon, Mr Hamilton flew over the border. He circled the defences of Juarez and reported the information he had gained to a border patrol.

Military authorities all over the world admit the value of aeroplanes for reconnoitring work and, although in Mr Hamilton's case the details of his flight are meagre, they serve, at any rate, to show the ease with which an airman can ascertain the position of the enemy's defences.

Captain Dickson during the Army manoeuvres on Salisbury Plain last autumn was officially attached to the Blue Army and he not only flew over the main body of the Red Army but, unaided by a passenger, was able to bring back information which the intelligence officers declared was "just what we wanted to know."

France has already a large fleet of aeroplanes in commission; Germany is busy both with aeroplanes and airships; and Russia lately gave an order to a British firm for six machines. The British War Office possesses at present only three or four aeroplanes, but it is believed that considerable additions will be made this year, and that more than a score of officers will be in constant training on Salisbury Plain.

8 March **1911**

WORLD'S AIR FLEETS

Air fleets of the world were discussed in the House of Commons yesterday when Mr Haldane, answering a question, said that France had four dirigibles completed and eight building while Russia had nine completed and one building. There was no definite information about German aeroplanes, added the War Minister. France had 70 available and Russia 10.

There were in the British Army nine officers and 108 non-commissioned officers and men being trained for air work. The Air Battalion would have a force of 14 officers and 176 of other ranks.

21 March **1911**

BRITAIN'S ROLE IN WORLD PEACE

A brisk contest over the question of whether Parliament should authorise the Government to maintain 134,000 men in the Navy took place in the House of Commons last night. The Government were vigorously peppered by some of their own men for allowing the Navy Estimates to jump up. Mr Thomas Lough – the white-haired, Irish-brogued member for West Islington – and Mr Hancock – the Labour member for Mid-Derbyshire – were among the pepperers.

"Germany does not want war," proclaimed Mr Hancock amid Unionist laughter, "and is making no preparation for war."

"If Germany is not preparing for war, what is she preparing for?" demanded Lord Charles Beresford. "I don't find any fault with Germany. Let them settle their own business. Our business is to see that no other nation destroys our Empire in consequence of our having lost command of the sea."

Lord Charles asked for an Imperial navy policy and severely criticised the Admiralty for having no war staff: "When war comes at sea it will be sudden, with everything organised by the enemy to attack our lines of food. That is our danger, and you have got to put cruisers on the trade routes ready for everything that might happen; if you don't, the food of the people is not secure."

KEEPING WORLD PEACE

"If we can get nations which make up the Empire and the United States to come together and throw in their power to try to influence all the other Powers on the side of peace, much can be done to delay war. You are never going to do away with war unless you are so well armed that the enemy cannot attack you."

31 March **1911**

GERMANY AND ARBITRATION

CHANCELLOR DECLARES THAT DISARMAMENT SCHEMES ARE UTTERLY IMPRACTICABLE

The Imperial Chancellor, Herr von Bethmann-Hollweg, pointed out in the Reichstag today that since disarmament was first mooted at The Hague Conference nobody had produced a practicable scheme.

Great Britain, in spite of her wish for disarmament, always insisted that her fleet must be equal or superior to any possible combination of Powers. How would a proposal for disarmament on such basis be received by a World Congress?

He was convinced in any case that all disarmament schemes must be wrecked on the question of control, which was utterly impracticable. Universal arbitration was as impossible as universal disarmament.

3 April **1911**

ANGLO-AMERICAN FRIENDSHIP

SIR R PERKS SAYS FORCES WOULD BE SIDE BY SIDE IN EVENT OF WAR

Sir Robert Perks, the well-known engineer, in an interview at New York's Hotel Saint Regis, said: "If Japan declared war against the United States the Anglo-Japanese treaty would not hold for five minutes. England is behind the United States and would array her forces by her side immediately."

Sir Robert added the opinion that there would be no war between Germany and England owing to the influence of commerce. Permanent peace, however, was impossible until Germany and England agreed to disarm.

17 July **1911**

➧ King George V inspects a naval guard of honour during a visit to Aberystwyth. The royal party was touring Wales following the investiture of the Prince of Wales.

25 September 1911

Naval airship HMA 1 *Mayfly*, was wrecked by a sudden squall while leaving her shed at Cavendish Dock at Barrow-in-Furness.

16 April 1912

EVERY ONE ON BOARD WORLD'S GREATEST LINER SAFE AFTER COLLISION WITH ICEBERG IN ATLANTIC OCEAN

TITANIC'S WIRELESS SIGNAL BRINGS VESSEL TO SCENE

46,000-ton Ship, with 2,300 Aboard in Peril.

EYERYONE SAFE

Morning of Suspense Ends in Message of Relief.

PASSENGERS TAKEN OFF

Helpless Giant Being Towed to Port by Allan Liner.

The White Star liner *Titanic*, the greatest ship the world has ever known, has met with disaster on her maiden voyage.

She left Southampton on Wednesday last and carried about 2,300 passengers and crew on board, with 3,400 sacks of mails.

On Sunday she came into collision with an iceberg, and immediately flashed out wireless messages for help.

Many steamers rushed to her aid, but her fate and that of the thousands on board remained in doubt on both sides of the Atlantic for many hours.

It was at length known that every soul was safe, and that the vessel itself was proceeding to Halifax (Nova Scotia), towed by the Allan liner *Virginian*.

All her passengers had by that time been taken aboard two of the liners that hurried to the scene in reply to the wireless message.

DRAMATIC TELEGRAMS OF DISASTER

So many and so conflicting were the reports that reached London yesterday concerning the fate of the *Titanic* that until detailed and definite tidings come to hand it is difficult to establish much more than the one all-important and outstanding fact that:

Every man, woman and child on the great liner is safe.

It would appear that once again the value to humanity of wireless telegraphy has been established, for at least five vessels are known to have hastened to the aid of the world's greatest ship when she flashed forth her appeal for help.

Three at least arrived in time to be of the greatest service, as is evident from the following series of dramatic Reuter messages which reached London yesterday at the times named (NB – New York time is five hours behind London):

6.15 am (New York) – A telegram received here from Montreal says:

"The liner *Virginian* reports in a wireless communication that the liner *Titanic*, which is reported to have been in collision with an iceberg, has requested assistance. The *Virginian* is hastening to her aid."

8.40 am (New York) – A telegram from Cape Race says:

"The wireless telegraph operator on board the *Titanic* reported the weather calm and clear, the position of the liner being then 41.46 north, 50.14 west.

"The *Virginian* at midnight was 170 miles west of the *Titanic*, and is expected to reach her at 10 o'clock this morning.

"The *Olympic* at midnight was in 40.32 north latitude, 61.18 west longitude. She is also in direct communication with the *Titanic*, and is hastening to her."

BLURRED MESSAGES

8.45 am (New York) – The liner *Baltic* has also reported herself within 200 miles of the *Titanic*, and says she is speeding to her help.

The last signals from the *Titanic* came at 12.27 this morning. The *Virginian*'s operator says that these were blurred and ended abruptly. – Reuter

9.50 am (New York) – A telegram from Cape Race says: "At 10.25 on Sunday evening the *Titanic* reported she had struck an iceberg. The steamer said that immediate assistance was required.

"Half an hour afterwards another message was received saying that the *Titanic* was sinking by the head, and that the women were being taken off in lifeboats." – Reuter

1.50 pm (New York) – Up to this hour the officials of the White Star Line have not received a word regarding the reported accident to the *Titanic*. The company have issued the following statement:

"Twelve hours have passed since the collision of the *Titanic* is reported to have taken place. We have heard nothing of an accident.

"It is very strange that the *Titanic*'s sister ship *Olympic*, which has a wireless installation of sufficient strength to send a message across the Atlantic, should have sent us nothing. The *Olympic* should be alongside the *Titanic* at two this afternoon."

2.58 pm (New York) – A dispatch from Halifax states that all the

The Daily Mirror

THE MORNING JOURNAL WITH THE SECOND LARGEST NET SALE.

No. 2,645. | Registered at the G.P.O. as a Newspaper. | TUESDAY, APRIL 16, 1912 | One Halfpenny.

DISASTER TO THE TITANIC: WORLD'S LARGEST SHIP COLLIDES WITH AN ICEBERG IN THE ATLANTIC DURING HER MAIDEN VOYAGE.

Disaster, it was reported yesterday, has overtaken the great steamer Titanic, the largest and most luxuriously appointed vessel afloat. The liner, which is the latest addition to the White Star fleet, left Southampton last Wednesday on her maiden voyage to New York, and was in the vicinity of the Newfoundland banks, to the south of Cape Race, when she struck an iceberg, an ever-present peril in those latitudes at this time of the year. "Wireless" has again demonstrated its immense value, assistance being summoned by this means. The photograph shows the mighty vessel leaving Southampton on Wednesday.—(*Daily Mirror* photograph.)

In a world where news travelled slowly things were often confused in the reportage. None more so than the fate of the *Titanic* in April 1912.

passengers of the *Titanic* had left the ship by 3.30 this morning.

3.50 pm (New York) – *The Montreal Star* reports from Halifax that the *Titanic* is still afloat and is making her way slowly to Halifax.

4.50 pm (New York) – A message from Montreal timed 8.30 am says:

"The *Titanic* is still afloat and heading towards Halifax.

"The women and children have not been taken off, though the lifeboats are ready in case of emergency. It is thought that the bulkheads will prevent her sinking."

A later message, says: "Wireless telegraphy brings the word that two vessels are standing by the *Titanic*, and that all the passengers have been taken off."

5.20 pm (New York) – "The transfer of the passengers from the *Titanic* is now being carried out. Twenty boat loads have already been taken on board the Cunarder *Carpathia*."

This last report was sent by wireless telegraphy to Mr Franklin, vice president of the White Star Company in New York, by Captain Haddock, of the *Olympic*, which is nearing the *Titanic*.

The dispatch adds that the *Parisian* and *Carpathia* are in attendance on the *Titanic*, and that the *Baltic* is nearing the ship.

Unofficial telegrams state that the *Virginian* has taken the *Titanic* in tow.

7.40 pm (New York) – Mr Franklin at one o'clock this afternoon gave out the following message received from the Boston office of the White Star Line:

"Allan line, Montreal, confirms report *Virginian*, *Parisian* and *Carpathia* in attendance, standing, by *Titanic*."

PASSENGERS TRANSHIPPED

Montreal, 15 April – It is now confirmed here that the passengers of the *Titanic* have been safely transhipped to the Allan liner *Parisian* and the Cunarder *Carpathia*. The *Virginian* is still towing the *Titanic* towards Halifax. – Exchange Telegraph

NO LIVES IN DANGER

New York, 15 April – The White Star officials here state that the *Virginian* is standing by the *Titanic* and that there is no danger of loss of life.

A wireless telegraph message to Halifax states that all the passengers were safely taken off the *Titanic* at 3.30.

Mr Franklin, vice president of the White Star Company, states that the *Titanic* is unsinkable. The fact that she was reported to have sunk several feet by the head was, he said, unimportant. She could go down many feet at the head as the result of water filling the forward compartments and yet remain afloat indefinitely.

STRUGGLING TOWARDS PORT

New York, 15 April – A wireless message received at Boston from St John's, Newfoundland, states that the *Titanic* is slowly struggling towards Cape Race. An unsigned wireless message, timed 8.30, has been received at Montreal, stating that the *Titanic* is still afloat, and is slowly steaming towards Halifax, Nova Scotia. The forward compartments are full of water, but if the vessel is able to withstand the strain it is hoped to make port.

News has now reached here that at 11.10 am (Canadian time) the local agents of the White Star Line at Montreal received another wireless message confirming the earlier reports that the *Titanic* was not only afloat but that the liner's engines were also working.

At this time the local agents were not aware whether the *Virginian* was with the *Titanic*, but they believed that she was standing by, and that possibly the women and children might have already been transferred. – Exchange Telegraph

LLOYD'S MESSAGE

According to a Lloyd's telegram, the signal station at Cape Race cabled yesterday as follows:

"10.25 pm yesterday (Sunday) the *Titanic* reports by wireless that she has struck an iceberg, and calls for immediate assistance. At 11 pm she was reported sinking by head. Women being put off in boats. Gave her position as 41.46 N., 50.14 W.

"Steamers *Baltic*, *Olympic*, and *Virginian* are all making towards the scene of the disaster. The latter was the last to hear the *Titanic*'s signals. At 12.27 am today (Monday) she reported them, then blurred and ending abruptly. It is believed that the *Virginian* will be the first ship to reach the *Titanic*."

WONDER OF WIRELESS

Thanks to the wonderful modern invention of wireless telegraphy, which 10 years ago was unknown, the *Titanic* was able to flash messages over the ocean asking for aid.

The wireless signal for "assistance wanted" is now "S.O.S.," the more familiar letters, "C.Q.D.," having been abandoned because they led to confusion with other code signals.

As a result of these "S.O.S." messages, five ships went to the assistance of the *Titanic* – the *Baltic* and the *Olympic*, of the White Star Line; the *Virginian* and the *Parisian*, of the Allan Line, and the Cunarder, *Carpathia*. The two last named took off boat-loads of passengers. Thus the passengers of the *Titanic* owe their safety to the invention of wireless, to the wondrous discovery of which it is due that every large liner is now in communication with any liner or battleship within hundreds of miles.

On the high seas in these days one has only, as it were, to touch a button to give the alarm and immediately there is a general rush to aid. The ocean, it may almost be said, is as well guarded as London by her fire brigade.

Every wireless operator on every ship has his ear glued eternally to the receiver, waiting for messages from the vasty deep. Suddenly taps out . . ., – – –, . . . , S.O.S. It spells out HELP. He is all alert to locate the sender of the message, and then the rush across the ocean on the errand of deliverance.

A marvellous picture this of man's battle with the weapons of science against the cruel forces of elemental nature.

23 July 1912

MR CHURCHILL ON NAVY PLANS FOR THE MEDITERRANEAN

In the House of Commons Mr Churchill last night expounded the new naval policy of the Government. But the First Lord's 80 minutes' speech fell on many of his hearers' ears in the light of an apology – he made plenty of promises, but gave us no new ships.

MEDITERRANEAN PLANS

The most eagerly-awaited part of the First Lord's speech was reserved till the end. This dealt, of course, with the Mediterranean. With emphatic gesture he denied that it was necessary for Britain to have a "local supremacy in the Mediterranean or elsewhere apart from its general sea supremacy."

What the Government had decided upon was this:

- ★ To station at Malta four battlecruisers of the Invincible class, taken from the North Sea.
- ★ To strengthen the squadron of four armoured cruisers now based on Malta by replacing its old ships with newer units.
- ★ To add to the submarine and destroyers flotillas at Malta.
- ★ A new torpedo station would be established at Alexandria.
- ★ To place at Gibraltar a squadron of eight battleships, two of which will be of very powerful type.
- ★ There will be no attempt to make the British force equal or superior to the combined Italian and Austrian units.

The right way to maintain our position in the Mediterranean, said the First Lord, was to maintain the smallest number of vessels which was good enough to do the work. It was not possible to settle the question merely on numbers. It would be necessary to add to the submarines at Malta.

The naval advisers of the Cabinet consider the arrangements the best possible under the circumstances, and satisfactory in themselves so far as the next two and a half years were concerned. It was not unlikely that the Mediterranean Squadron might have to be reinforced towards the end of 1916.

GERMANY'S RAPID ADVANCE

There were many other notable features in the First Lord's speech, which was closely followed by a thronged and distinguished House.

Here are some outstanding points:

- ★ A significant allusion to the increase in striking force of the ships of all classes of the German Navy, four-fifths of these vessels to be in full permanent equipment and instantly ready for war.
- ★ The increase of naval strength in the Mediterranean by Austria and Italy.
- ★ Canada's offer to strengthen the naval forces of the Empire.

Germany was spending about a million pounds a year on submarines, and we must not allow our expenditure to be diminished, and while we were spending £60,000 a year on aircraft, Germany was spending £100,000. The increase of the striking force of the German Navy involved a considerable reorganisation of the British Fleet in order to maintain a margin of safety of ships in full commission.

➧ Winston Churchill, First Lord of the Admiralty, with Lord Fisher at the Yarrow shipyard for the launch of HMS *Marlborough* in November 1911.

In the face of rising world tension, the Coronation of George V and Queen Mary gave the public an opportunity to celebrate, 22 June 1911.

Thousands of people cheer from the side of the roads as the Coronation procession makes its way through London, 22 June 1911.

◀ King George V and Queen Mary visit India in January 1912.

▼ The King and Queen are transported by horse and cart during their visit to Calcutta, 1912.

The Turco-Italian War was fought between the Ottoman Empire and the Kingdom of Italy from 29 September 1911 to 18 October 1912. As a result of this conflict, Italy captured the Ottoman provinces of Tripolitania, Fezzan and Cyrenaica. These provinces together formed what became known as Libya.

Although minor, the war was significant in the context of the First World War as it sparked nationalism in the Balkan states. It also saw numerous technological advances used in warfare, notably the airplane. On 23 October 1911, an Italian pilot, Captain Carlo Piazza, flew over Turkish lines on the world's first aerial reconnaissance mission, and on 1 November, the first ever aerial bomb was dropped by Sottotenente Giulio Gavotti, on Turkish troops in Libya. The Turks, lacking anti-aircraft weapons, were the first to shoot down an aeroplane by rifle fire.

Another Crisis in the Balkans

26 September **1912** – 2 December **1912**

Despite several prominent European nations attempting to prevent the outbreak of war in the Balkans, conflict did arise with Bulgaria, Greece, Montenegro and Servia taking on the might of the Ottoman Empire. This was brought to a close in May 1913 with the Treaty of London but Bulgaria's dissatisfaction with her spoils led to a second war between June and July 1913.

This time, hostilities did break out between several of the Balkan States, resulting in a crisis that again threatened to descend Europe into war. Soldiers sit in a carriage with huge guns and artillery on the way to Adrianople, Turkey, in November 1912.

RUMANIA
BOSNIA
SERVIA
BULGARIA
MONTE-
NEGRO
TURKEY
GREECE
ASIA
MINOR

26 September **1912**

MENACE OF WAR IN THE BALKANS

NATIONS ARMING

Again the Balkans are aflame with war fever and recent events, described by the Austrian Foreign Minister as "a display of sheet lightning", show that the unrest, often acute, is fast approaching the danger point.

Bulgaria is eager to be at the throat of the Turk. Her people, eager for war, have so far been restrained by the King and Government but now, secure in the support of the Slav nationalities, she has suddenly stopped her manoeuvres and is hurriedly bringing her army up to a war footing.

Moreover, Bulgaria is said to have concluded an offensive alliance against Turkey with Servia, Greece and Montenegro, who are said to be arming.

Turkey is preparing for her defence and the reserves are being raised to full strength.

NATIONS IN CONFLICT

The Balkan States, which take their name from the Balkan Mountains, are five in number – Turkey (in Europe), Bulgaria, Romania, Servia and Montenegro – although it should be noted that Turkey's population includes 1,500,000 hostile Albanians and 1,300,000 Greeks, Bulgarians and Wallachians.

The real trouble began in the last Administration of Lord Beaconsfield, when Mr Gladstone, in his famous campaign, stirred up English animosity against the Turks and encouraged Christian nationalities to fight for "liberty and independence" against the Turkish yoke.

The Servians were first to respond and, when they were beaten, Russia stepped in to save Servia and declared war on Turkey. The result of that was the Treaty of St Stefano which practically began the partition of Turkey on the lines now aimed at by the Nationalists in Turkey.

It left Turkey the rule of little more than Constantinople and a limited sweep of the territory beyond it.

England, however, could not consent to such a violent breaking up of Turkey as it would place Constantinople practically at the mercy of Russia, the patron of the southern Slav kingdoms.

Ever since, the Balkan States have been spending much of their money and most of their energy in preparation for war with Turkey.

30 September **1912**

BULGARIAN TROOPS FOR FRONTIER

SEVEN COUNTRIES PREPARING ARMIES FOR THE FIELD

It needs but a spark to explode the Balkan powder magazine, for all the elements of a tremendous explosion are ready. During the week, seven European armies were being prepared for mobilisation or calling up reserves. Here, briefly, are the preparations made:

- ⋆ Austria – reserves called up and with the colours.
- ⋆ Russia – eight army corps mobilised in Warsaw and district "as a test".
- ⋆ Italy – first-class reserves of 1890 and 1887 now on leave recalled to colours.
- ⋆ Turkey – 200,000 troops ready near Bulgarian frontier.
- ⋆ Bulgaria – army mobilised ready for war. Railways refusing civil transport.
- ⋆ Servia – War Office busy. Eighteen carloads of Turkish ammunition detrained at Belgrade. Some recruits called up.
- ⋆ Greece – mobilisation reported begun.

BULGARIA'S THREAT

The relations between the National Bank and the Ottoman Bank have been broken off. Troops from the capital are being dispatched to the frontier. Three divisions of troops are to be formed at Sliven, Kustendil and Sarazagora.

The Bulgarian Government, in the event of Turkey refusing to withdraw her troops from Adrianople, will, it is reported, inform the Powers of her intention to immediately order a general mobilisation.

"WILL END IN WAR"

The fear is growing in unofficial circles that the present critical situation will end in war being declared between Servia and Turkey, all the necessary preparations for which are said to have been effected.

To avoid any undue sensation, however, the reserves have been called up in small numbers and sent to their regiments on the Turco-Servian frontier. The movements of Turkish troops on the frontier are causing the greatest uneasiness among the local officials.

RUSSIA'S STRANGE MOVE

Military authorities of the Warsaw district ordered a partial mobilisation of the troops in their district, and also in the Wilua and Kieff districts. The corps which have been mobilised are the 2nd, 6th, 9th, 14th, 15th, 19th, 20th and 23rd Army Corps.

Although the mobilisation is officially described as being carried out as a test, the complete unexpectedness of such an order has made an enormous impression throughout the country, the greater since no test-mobilisation has been carried out in Warsaw for a number of years.

2 October **1912**

BALKAN LEAGUE AGAINST TURKEY

The situation in the Balkans could hardly be more threatening. The only hopeful factor is that the Great Powers of the Triple Entente and the Triple Alliance are working strenuously for peace. Behind the veil that obscures the working of international diplomacy tremendous efforts, it is known, are being made to avert a Balkan outbreak.

But, apart from this, the situation grew steadily worse yesterday. Montenegro joined Bulgaria, Servia and Greece in ordering a mobilisation of her forces and the Prime Ministers of the latter three States definitely stated that they were acting in unison against Turkey.

In Servia tremendous military activity prevailed – troop trains ran all night, all motor cars were commandeered and so many men were called up to join the army that the trains were without men to work them and business had to close for the same purpose.

The King of Greece is hurrying back to Athens; Bulgaria – as, indeed, are all the three allied States – is calling back officers and men liable to service from abroad; Montenegro is aflame with war fever; it needs but a spark to start the Balkan conflagration.

And Turkey, rent with internal troubles, still striving to suppress the insurgents in Macedonia, was preparing with Oriental secrecy, drawing on her great reserves of men to meet the conflict that seemed almost inevitable. Peace is almost impossible, declared the Bulgarian Minister in Paris yesterday.

Turkish troops on the march, October 1912.

Servian troops march through Uskub, November 1912.

Turkish children salute Servian soldiers.

Turkish cavalry riding towards the front of the column in Constantinople.

Turkish refugees retreat to Constantinople as the Balkan Wars intensify, November 1912.

▲ Bernard Grant, *Daily Mirror* photographer in late October 1912 (left with fez), who was embedded with the Turkish Army during the Balkan Wars and took the photos on this and the preceding page.

◀ A young Bulgarian soldier on the march during the Bulgarian pursuit of the Turkish Army.

▶ Bulgarians firing on the retreating Turkish Army, November 1912.

8 October 1912

PROBLEM OF THE NATIONS

WHAT EUROPE WANTS NOW

To prevent war, or failing that, to localise the conflict. To secure reforms in Macedonia, while safeguarding Turkey's interests.

WHAT TURKEY WANTS

To keep Macedonia and her other provinces without going to the length of granting them autonomy. To avoid war by granting some reforms, but not all that the Balkan States demand. To avoid giving such reforms as may encourage provinces to revolt, as Eastern Rumalia did.

BULGARIA, SERVIA, MONTENEGRO

To get complete home rule for Macedonia and Albania. Also, sooner or later, to add part of these provinces to their own dominions – but not by their present action.

GREECE

To secure the union of Crete to Greece and reforms in Macedonia. Also, ultimately more territory at Turkey's expense.

AUSTRIA

At present maintain the status quo and prevent the Balkan States or Russia from acquiring more territory. Ultimately possession of the port of Salonika and territory leading to it – Novibazar and part of Macedonia.

WHAT RUSSIA WANTS

To secure the opening of the Dardanelles and prevent Austria getting any of the present Turkish territory.

WHAT MACEDONIA WANTS

Liberty of person and reforms, including self-government. To be free of the Turkish rule.

8 November 1912

ALBANIA A KINGDOM

TRIPLE ALLIANCE BARRING WAY OF SERVIA TO ADRIATIC

A remarkable report that Austria and Germany have agreed with Italy to set up an independent kingdom in Albania with the Duke of the Abruzzi as ruler, comes from Berlin. The Italian Foreign Minister's conferences in Berlin have had the following results:

- The Powers of the Triple Alliance (Germany, Austria and Italy) have agreed that Albania shall become an independent kingdom under the Duke of the Abruzzi, cousin of the King of Italy.

- It is believed that this has been decided upon in view of the fact that the King of Italy supports Austria's claim to Salonica.

- Durazzo, the port on the Adriatic for which Servia is making a

bold bid, is in Albania. Servian troops are already reported to be advancing in that direction. The situation, therefore, is full of grave dangers.

11 November **1912**

"MAP OF EUROPE HAS TO BE RECAST"

FRUITS OF VICTORY

The victors are not to be robbed of the fruits that cost them so dear.

In that phrase, which occurs in Mr Asquith's Guildhall speech, you have the crux of the whole position – the foundation of peace or the cause of a European war.

Such was the comment passed in a conversation with *The Daily Mirror* yesterday by a famous diplomatist who is well versed in European politics.

"Mr Asquith's speech was unmistakably clear and bold. It can only mean one thing and that is, come what may, the Balkan States will be supported by Great Britain in whatever demands they may reasonably make for the recasting of the map of Europe.

"Servia has always longed for an outlet in the Adriatic Sea for commercial purposes, and she now considers she had established her right to such an outlet by her victories over the Turks in Albania.

"But Austria has always shown herself strenuously opposed to any widening of Servia's boundaries, and what I fear is that she will insist on robbing Servia of the 'fruits of victory'.

"What follows? Italy and Germany side with Austria against Servia, and then you have the prospect of the Triple Alliance opposed to the Triple Entente – Great Britain, France and Russia.

"Undoubtedly the situation is a very delicate and a very grave one."

Winston Churchill and his wife Clementine arrive for the launching of HMS *Iron Duke* in 1912.

27 November **1912**

EUROPEAN WAR CLOUD LIFTING

POWERS MAY YET FIND A WAY OUT OF CRISIS

It is impossible to overrate the gravity of the situation in Europe. It is possible, at the same time, to be somewhat optimistic as to the issue.

Behind the diplomats at the Chancelleries of the Powers, who are playing the mighty game of war and peace, are millions of commonsense ordinary people – Austrians, Russians, Germans, Englishmen, Frenchmen and Italians – who do not want war, who have no impulse to go to war.

It would seem inconceivable that six great civilised nations should go to war because an infant State wants a port on the Adriatic Sea, and the feeling is growing that because of the sheer folly of plunging a Continent into Armageddon, of which none can foresee the issue, war will be avoided.

The Arms Race

3 December **1912** – 27 June **1914**

By this time, Great Britain had serious reservations regarding the increase in size of Germany's Navy. Add in the rapid introduction of airships and fledgling flying machines to the military equation and it was no wonder that both countries were spending more and more each year trying to equip their forces in anticipation of conflict.

HMS *Audacious*, a King George V-class battleship built for the Royal Navy at Cammell Laird from 1911 to 1913. One year after her commissioning, *Audacious* put to sea from her base at Lough Swilly for target practice, along with the other battleships of the 2nd Battle Squadron. While passing Tory Island the vessel struck a mine and began to take on water.

3 December **1912**

GERMANY'S POSITION MADE CLEAR

WOULD FIGHT IF AUSTRIA WERE ATTACKED BY A THIRD POWER

A significant statement was made yesterday by the German Chancellor – a statement of so great import that it may definitely prevent a general war in Europe. Dr von Bethmann-Hollweg made it clear that while Germany would remain an onlooker in the event of an Austro-Servian conflict, if a third Power were to attack Austria, Germany would fight by her side and, he was convinced, would have the whole of the German people behind her.

This means only one thing. If Russia comes to Servia's aid and crosses the Austrian frontier, Germany will immediately take the offensive against Russia.

So tremendous are the issues, in fact, that, with Germany's attitude made irrevocably plain, Russia must needs hesitate before listening to the Pan-Slav voice prompting her to support Servia against her Teutonic neighbour.

Winston Churchill and General Sir John French observe military manoeuvres on Salisbury Plain, Winter 1912.

14 February **1913**

BRITAIN HELPLESS AGAINST AIR FOE

DEFENCE "ALMOST WORTHLESS" TO SAVE SEA FLEET FROM SKY BOMBS

"If Germany declared war against Great Britain tomorrow we should be beaten."

This grave statement is not the ill-considered view of an alarmist, but the impartial opinion of one of the most expert students of naval warfare – a man whose soundness of judgment has been frequently acknowledged by the best authorities. It was with this striking sentence that he summed up for *The Daily Mirror* yesterday the present relative position of Great Britain and Germany in regard to airships and aeroplanes and their effect on the next naval war.

The same serious view is also taken by an able writer in the "Review of Reviews".

"The sea to us, the air to the foe", is how he tersely sums up Britain's peril in the air.

"With all our Dreadnoughts," he says, "this country is today as defenceless before foreign attack as at any time in our history.

"All the world knows that German airships can come at any moment, without any risk or peril other than those of the elements, to do what they will, when and how they may decide, in any part of the country.

"No secret is made in Germany of the radius of action and capabilities of the new German airships. The German L1, the best airship in the world, has covered 800 miles over land and sea in its trials, has a carrying capacity of 27 tons, and a radius of action of 1,550 miles, with a speed of 50 miles an hour."

27 March **1913**

"NAVAL HOLIDAY FOR A YEAR"

MR CHURCHILL'S STRIKING OFFER TO GERMANY

A "naval holiday for a year" – a period in which none of the Powers should build any ships – this was the striking suggestion put forward by Mr Winston Churchill in introducing the Navy Estimates in the House of Commons last night. Other features of the First Lord's eagerly awaited statement were:

* An Imperial squadron, consisting of five capital ships, to be formed; this to be stationed at Gibraltar, so as to be able to reach quickly any part of the British Empire.

* The 60 percent standard of superiority to be maintained over Germany.

* The British programme to be increased by four capital ships in view of Germany's increase of two capital ships, two of the British ships to be laid down this year.

* The vessels given by the Malay States and Canada to be regarded as additional to the Home programme.

* The Admiralty have been in communication with ship owners as

to arming merchant ships, and have arranged to lend the necessary guns, provide ammunition and train ships' companies to form gun crews.

* There will be 100 pilots and 100 air machines at the end of the financial year – altogether 300 aeroplanes between the Navy and the Army.

Marcus Manton in a Grahame-White biplane used for Lewis gun tests in 1913.

31 March **1913**

GERMANY'S GREAT AIR FLEET

30 MORE AIRSHIPS AND 250 MORE AEROPLANES PROVIDED FOR

A remarkable response has been made by Germany to Mr Churchill's proposal for a year's naval holiday. In round figures a capital sum of £7,000,000 is to be spent within the next five years in providing new and greater air fleets for the Army and Navy.

Thirty new airships are to be added to the 12 Germany already possesses and 250 new aeroplanes to the existing 150 – 200 being for the Army and 50 for the Navy.

28 May **1913**

King George V, accompanied by his cousin Kaiser Wilhelm II of Germany, pictured visiting the German Regiment of the First Dragoon Guards on his visit to Berlin in May 1913.

6 June **1913**

BRITAIN'S PLACE IN THE AIR

COLONEL SEELY CLAIMS WE HAVE MADE BIG ADVANCE IN A YEAR

Is Great Britain's progress in aircraft satisfactory? This was the question which for the greater part of an hour Colonel Seely, the Minister for War, sought to answer in the affirmative in the House of Commons last night. The main features of his speech were the following:

* A refusal to divulge the exact numbers and types of aircraft we possess. "No foreign country gives these figures," he pleaded.

Winston Churchill with the Kaiser and a German officer, 1913.

HAIR
DRESSING
SALOON
HAIR
CUTTING
SHAVING
SALOON
FENDICK
LENNARD
TAILOR

Charing Cross Road in London after Miss Sylvia Pankhurst was re-arrested and taken to Charing Cross Police Station, Spring 1913.

★ An invitation to Mr Joynson-Hicks, his critic, to inspect 80 aeroplanes and fly in them.

★ An assurance that the problem of invasion is one we can "contemplate without fear".

★ A statement that for nine and a half years he had held the view that compulsory service would be a political and military disaster.

7 August 1913

PEACE AT LAST IN THE BALKANS

RUMANIA'S THREAT TO BULGARIA BRINGS HER TO TERMS

War in the Balkans is at an end at last. Telegrams from Bucharest last night announced that peace had been concluded between Bulgaria and her enemies, Servia, Greece and Montenegro, who were afterwards joined by Rumania, as a result of their quarrels over the spoils of victory gained in the long drawn out fight with Turkey.

Peace will be signed today, and orders for demobilisation issued. According to these terms, Greece is to have Kavala, the important seaport on the Aegean Sea behind the island of Thasos.

Bulgaria will have a frontier following, roughly, the lines of the Strunia and Mesta rivers, in Macedonia, and giving her the towns of Strumnitza and Xanthi and the port of Lagos on the Aegean. She leaves the conference hoping that by the later action of the Great Powers she will yet – a depressed and weakened nation – get something more.

War has existed in the Balkans since October last, when Bulgaria, Servia, Greece and Montenegro began their successful campaign against Turkey.

The quarrels among the Allies took definite shape towards the end of May last.

9 January 1914

➧ The 4th London Royal Fusiliers have arranged to have "The Life of a Soldier" film shown on the screen at the Angel cinema. After the screening several recruiting sergeants accost likely looking men who have seen the film, with the view to enlisting them. This picture shows the recruiting sergeants talking to prospective recruits but little did the men who signed up at the beginning of 1914 know that eight months later they would be thrown into the First World War.

28 February **1914**

"FOR SAFETY OF THESE ISLANDS"

NAVY CAPABLE AS EVER

"Let the people once realise that there is a very real danger and they will readily adopt any system that may be found necessary to protect them."

These outspoken words of warning used by Lord Roberts, great soldier and patriot, formed the keynote of an influential deputation of the National Service League, which waited upon Mr Asquith yesterday to urge the necessity for the adoption of a system of compulsory military training.

Mr Asquith, in his reply, said that the Territorial Force was improving. A sub-committee of the Committee of Imperial Defence had practically adopted a unanimous report, which he thought would have great weight.

He could not, said Mr Asquith, anticipate that report, except to say that he was sure the conclusions would not support the view that the Navy was not as capable as it had ever been in protecting the country from anything in the nature of a serious invasion.

"ALL SIDES PREPARING FOR WAR"

In his warning of a "very real danger", Lord Roberts, introducing the deputation, said:

"The Territorial Force is but little better fitted for the special duty for which it was established than were the displaced Volunteers.

"The present Government, like their predecessors, allow the nation to believe that, so long as we possess a powerful Navy, an invasion of these islands is an impossibility, and therefore there is no need for an efficient land force.

"I can quite understand the people not caring for universal military training, because they do not understand the benefit to be derived from it."

Lord Roberts said they saw on all sides continued and increasing preparation for war. They were brought face to face with a state of affairs which required prompt action.

Sir James Crichton-Browne, who among others supported Lord Roberts, said military drill and discipline among adolescence would improve the physique of people and enlarge their mental calibre. It would do much to counteract hooliganism.

Mr Asquith, in reply said the deputation had urged that "the immunity from invasion, which it was once believed our Navy could afford no longer exists"; and they went on to say: "The result of these developments if that in the considered words of the First Sea Lord the Navy alone cannot now protect the country from invasion."

Mr Asquith said he was desired by the First Sea Lord, Prince Louis of Battenberg, to repudiate these words, and that the meaning attached to them rested on a misconstruction.

Answering Lord Roberts' contention that the "Territorial Force was but little better fitted for the special duty for which it was established than were the displaced Volunteers", Mr Asquith said that:

"with the exception of Lord Roberts he had never heard any distinguished and experienced officer deny that the Territorial Force, with all its defects and shortcomings, was a vast improvement on the Volunteer Force."

Looking to the condition and equipment of our Navy on one side, and to our home forces on the other, he saw no adequate ground for the apprehensions the deputation expressed.

3 March **1914**

BRITAIN'S BID FOR GREAT SKY NAVY

£250,000 AIR FLEET

★ One large and three smaller non-rigid airships ordered in England.

★ One large airship ordered in France.

★ Three large airships, of an Italian semi-rigid design, ordered.

These details of the nucleus of a great fleet of airships for Britain were announced yesterday by Mr Winston Churchill, First Lord of the Admiralty, in the House of Commons.

A vision of Britain's future with a great navy of giant war machines, oil-driven and supplemented by a strong air fleet of warplanes and armed airships, was outlined by Mr Churchill when the House went into committee on the Naval Supplementary Estimates and discussed a vote of £2,500,000.

A considerable programme of airship construction had been approved, and new contracts had been made, he said, which would be executed as fast as possible.

COAST DEFENCE BY AIR

The first cause of the increase, Mr Churchill explained, was expenditure on oil reserve – £500,000 was represented by that. The second cause was the programme of aircraft costing £250,000 in the present year.

The third cause was an increase in wages in dockyards and in the price of victuals and clothing. This accounted for little short of £200,000.

The fourth cause was the expenditure of £450,000 on the acceleration of and the beginning earlier of three battleships of the 1913–14 programme to cover the temporary delay in the passage of the Canadian Naval Aid Bill.

The fifth cause was the better progress which had been made by contractors in shipyards all over the country. That explained the need for an extra million pounds.

The growing cost of twin fleets, air and sea, was then explained by Mr Churchill.

The average price of oil, he said, had more than doubled in the last two years. They now had safely stored in this country more than three years' peace consumption for the whole of our existing very large oil-burning fleet.

The air service, Mr Churchill went on, had now reached a point – though still in its experimental stage – when it had begun to share the military responsibilities of the Navy. It was about to become an effective factor in naval operations and coast defence.

The chief expense under aircraft was for airships, airship-sheds and stores. A considerable new programme of airship construction had been approved, and contracts had been made which would be executed as fast as possible.

It had been considered necessary to interest British contractors in the manufacture of airships.

"LATE IN STARTING, BUT . . ."

One large and three smaller non-rigid airships had been ordered from Messrs Vickers. Another large airship had been ordered in France. A contract had been signed with Armstrongs for three large airships of an Italian semi-rigid design.

They were late in starting the British air service, both by sea and land, said Mr Churchill, but their tardiness in airship construction would ultimately be fully justified.

Great progress had been made in every direction. The total cost of the eight new airships and sheds would be approximately £475,000, and of this £200,000 would fall on the present year. This, with the additional expenditure on seaplanes brought the total up to £260,000.

There was a vast volume of shipbuilding in the shipyards of the country. It included 14 great ships, 62 smaller vessels of various kinds, besides numerous submarines. Several members criticised the Estimates, and Mr D Mason moved a reduction on account of the unconstitutional action of the Admiralty in spending money before it was sanctioned by Parliament.

The motion was defeated by 237 votes to 34. The debate was adjourned.

11 March **1914**

The training ship *Wellesley* was destroyed by fire on the River Tyne in March 1914. The ship was part of the Wellesley Nautical School founded in 1868 and was aimed to train young men for service at sea. She was the last of the wooden battleships and originally called HMS *Boscawen*.

K6

13 March **1914**

FIRST LORD ASKS FOR £51,550,000

BOMB WARFARE BY FLEET OF SEAPLANES – NEW AIRSHIP STATIONS

* 4 battleships
* 4 light cruisers
* 12 destroyers
* A number of submarines
* 5,000 extra officers and men
* £51,550,000 – total required

These are the important features of the Navy Estimates for the ensuing year which were issued last night. The estimates reach a record total of £51,550,000, a net increase upon the 1913–14 estimates of £2,740,700.

The cost of the new programme – battleships, light cruisers, destroyers, submarines and increased personnel given above in detail – will amount to nearly £15,000,000.

Britain's other fleet – of seaplanes and airships – is also being rapidly perfected and, Mr Churchill points out, a chain of seaplane bases is being placed around the coast.

Submarine K6, one of the K-class steam-propelled submarines of the Royal Navy designed in 1913. Intended as large, fast vessels that would operate with the battle fleet, they gained notoriety, and the nickname of Kalamity class, for being involved in many accidents. Of the 18 built none were lost through enemy action but six sank in accidents. Only one ever engaged an enemy vessel, hitting a U-boat amidships, though the torpedo failed to explode.

COAST CHAIN OF SEAPLANE BASES

An interesting glimpse of how aeroplanes and airships are being adapted for war purposes is given by Mr Churchill in his statement.

Seaplanes have combined for war exercises with the patrol and defence flotillas, and also took part in the naval manoeuvres in July, and a flight of naval aeroplanes was employed during Army manoeuvres.

A cruiser was specially commissioned and fitted out to carry seaplanes, and in consequence of the experience gained in this ship it has been decided to procure a special seaplane-carrying ship.

Progress has been made in the establishment of a chain of seaplane bases round the coast; five stations are completed, and the formation of others is proceeding.

BOMBS FROM SEAPLANES

Good progress has been made with the design of the seaplane itself, and its development into certain standard types for war purposes is rapidly proceeding.

The practical utility of aeroplanes and seaplanes for war purposes is increasingly evident, and the experiments in connection with bomb dropping, wireless telegraphy and gunnery have been continuous.

At certain bases around the coast the personnel of the air service have replaced the coastguard and are carrying out coastguard duties in addition to naval air station work.

As the air service develops it is hoped that a considerable number of the coastguard stations may be transferred and economies therefore effected.

Good progress has also been made in the development of airships. The Astra Torres and Parseval airships ordered last year have been successful and further orders for ships of this type have been placed.

LARGEST AIRSHIP SHEDS

The establishment of an airship station on the Medway with two sheds of the largest size is being pressed forward, and should be completed shortly. A site for another station has been procured, and the establishment of an inland airship station for training purposes is under construction.

Arrangements have been made to transfer the Army airships to the Admiralty, and in future all airship work will be carried out by the Navy.

14 March **1914**

NO NEED FOR WAR SCARE

Berlin, 13 March – A sensational article appears in the newspaper *Germania*, which alleges that Russia is mobilising. Prominent Russians strongly deny the statement that Russia is preparing for war, and the Russian Foreign Minister, M Sazonoff, has declared that the increase in armaments was started by Germany, Russia being thus bound to take steps for herself. Her army, she says, is being developed – but in the interests of peace.

18 March **1914**

SKY NAVY TO SAIL OVER BIG BEN

"IF THERE WERE WAR . . ."

"I will bring half a dozen airships for a cruise over the House during the session," was the picturesque vow made by Mr Churchill in the House of Commons yesterday in the course of his speech on the new Navy Estimates – "the largest estimates ever presented."

He would do this, he said, to show members that they were really in existence. With regard to Britain's air fleet, Mr Churchill said the Government's policy was that this country should be masters of its own air. They had – built, building and ordered – 15 airships, of which three were large vessels.

The growth of the aerial navy from 1911 (when Mr Churchill assumed office) to the present day was as follows:

THEN	NOW
4 aeroplanes	43 aeroplanes
5 pilots	62 seaplanes
	120 regular pilots
	20 officers with Aero Club certificate
	6 land stations around the coast
	2 stations under construction

The seaplane, Mr Churchill said, had a great future, and in this department of aeronautics we were far before any other country. The airship service would form the second stage in the career of flying officers, as aeroplanes were only suitable for the use of young men.

The three principal causes of the increase of £2,740,700 on last year's estimate of £48,809,200 were oil, air and personnel.

Important reference was made to German naval construction. In regard to this Mr Churchill's outstanding observation was:

"It would have been possible for us to have completed our development at a somewhat earlier period than we now propose to do, but the development of the German fleet organisation has not been so rapid as I anticipated two years ago."

THE RIVAL FLEETS

At the end of this year we should have 33 battleships in full commission against Germany's 25, with 16 battleships in reserve, Germany having an equal number in reserve.

Then we had a second fleet of 16 battleships against which there was no corresponding item in the German Navy.

If war broke out tomorrow every ship could be sent out with its full complement.

The personnel of the Navy was now 146,000, as against 133,717 in 1911, and he now asked for an increase of 5,000.

The Admiralty regarded the effort of Australia to establish a fleet as heroic.

Mr Churchill suggested the formation of an imperial squadron, the capital ships of which could move rapidly all over the world.

25 June **1914**

HAS SERVIAN KING ABDICATED?

CROWN PRINCE APPOINTED TO GOVERN DURING MONARCH'S ILLNESS

Has King Peter of Servia abdicated in favour of the Crown Prince Alexander? A message from Belgrade yesterday definitely stated that he had taken this step and added a proclamation would be issued immediately, explaining that His Majesty's action is taken on the ground of continued ill-health. The proclamation, however, as given in a later message reads thus:

"To My Beloved People: As I shall be prevented by illness from exercising my royal power for some time, I order, by Artickel 69 of the Constitution, that so long as my cure lasts the Crown Prince Alexander shall govern in my name. On this occasion I recommend my dear fatherland to the care of the Almighty. Signed Peter".

The proclamation is countersigned by the whole body of Ministers. This is the first time since his accession that King Peter had handed over the Government to the Crown Prince during his visits to baths in Servia for a cure.

The Skupstina was dissolved yesterday, and the new elections have been ordered for 14 August.

FAMILY THAT RULES BY SWORD

After 11 years of troublesome rule of one of the most turbulent people in Europe, King Peter has relinquished his task. He has left his semi-European capital of Belgrade and is taking the waters in a small inland resort near what was once the Macedonian frontier. Thus ends probably what was one of the most tragically picturesque, and at times sordid, stories of the Balkans.

It out-distances by far the imagination of Ruritanian novelists. King Peter was a descendant of Black George, swineherd, bandit and fighting man, who seized the throne of the Servian peoples by the strength of his own hand.

His family likewise were compelled to rule by the sword until the rival shepherd family of Obrenovitch came along and thrust Black George into the more or less pleasant exile of Paris and Monte Carlo.

CITY OF PLOTTERS

Belgrade then was, and it still is, and probably always will be, a city of plotters. In every one of the hundreds of little cafés men and women would plot in favour of rival dynasties until that terrible tragic night of 10 June 1903, when King Alexander and Queen Draga were murdered in their beds by drunken assassins, who showed no pity for the followers of the King to whom they had sworn allegiance.

For five days Belgrade was a city of turmoil and drawn daggers. No one dared speak, no one dared write. Five days afterwards Peter, who was waiting in Paris, was elected King of Servia and duly crowned the following year.

For five years Great Britain declined to recognise his existence. Until the outbreak of war against the Turks two years ago King Peter hardly knew from day to day whether he would remain on the throne. Her sons, the army, politicians and supporters of the rival dynasty were constantly plotting against him, now supported by financiers, now by Austria or by Turkey, and often by Russia.

With the war came a change of feeling in Servia. That was King Peter's hey-day. He was popular, he was cheered. His throne was secure. He was friendly once again with his sons.

FEAR OF THE KING-MAKER

But the influence of the war did not last for long. The army officers, who play a very great role in the government of the country and securing of prizes, were disgusted to find that the major share of the good things that were "going" went to the politicians. They complained time after time to the King, but he was unable to satisfy them.

For to satisfy them would have been to offend M Pasitch, the Prime Minister and the king-maker of Servia.

M Pasitch is now an old man, with a venerable white beard, but his word is, and has been, law in Servia ever since the day when King Alexander was murdered, and M Pasitch was determined that the army should not get the upper hand in Servia.

Whenever the army opposed him in Parliament he tendered his resignation, and without him King Peter was helpless, and the King knew it.

The Dreadnoughts HMS *Superb* and HMS *Lion* at anchor in Lamlash Bay off of Arran, May 1914.

The Trigger is Pulled

28 June **1914** – 27 July **1914**

The assassination of Archduke Francis Ferdinand and his wife in Sarajevo has long been seen as the catalyst for the origins of the First World War but, while it was certainly a major factor, it was the defining moment that set Austria-Hungary against Servia. Naturally, their allies stood by them and the rest is history . . .

◀ It was impossible to forecast the scale of the conflict that would engulf the world between 1914 and 1918 which would leave more than 16 million people dead and 20 million wounded.

THE DAILY MIRROR, Monday, June 29, 1914.

Aged Austrian Emperor Loses His Nephew at an Assassin's Hand

The Daily Mirror

LATEST CERTIFIED CIRCULATION MORE THAN 960,000 COPIES PER DAY

No. 3,332. Registered at the G.P.O. as a Newspaper. MONDAY, JUNE 29, 1914 One Halfpenny.

HEIR TO THE AUSTRIAN THRONE AND HIS WIFE SHOT DEAD IN STREET AT SERAJEVO AFTER BOMB HAD FAILED.

The Duchess of Hohenberg.

The Archduke Francis Ferdinand.

The Archduke, his wife and their family.

Another assassination in the history of the unhappy House of Hapsburg occurred yesterday, when the Archduke Francis Ferdinand, heir to the throne of Austria, and his wife, the Duchess of Hohenberg, were shot dead as they were leaving the railway station at Serajevo, the capital of Bosnia. The fatal shots were fired by an eighteen-year-old Servian student who had been banished from Bosnia. Before firing the revolver another assassin had flung a bomb into the carriage, but it failed to explode.

29 June **1914**

AUSTRIAN HEIR ASSASSINATED

ARCHDUKE FRANCIS FERDINAND AND HIS WIFE SHOT DEAD IN STREET

The Archduke Francis Ferdinand, heir to the throne of Austria-Hungary, and the Duchess of Hohenberg, his morganatic wife, were assassinated yesterday at Sarajevo. This terrible news, which has shocked all Europe, reached London last night from Vienna.

Two deliberate and cold-blooded attempts, it appears from the telegraphed accounts of the tragedy, were made. First a bomb was thrown at the Archduke's carriage as he was driving with his wife through the streets of Sarajevo, the capital of Bosnia. This dastardly attack failed, but several spectators were injured.

Then, while the Archduke was continuing his drive, a student suddenly levelled a Browning pistol and fired. With deadly aim he first shot the Archduke and then, turning the weapon, mortally injured the Duchess.

Once again the red hand of the assassin plunged the tragic House of Hapsburg into mourning.

The man who threw the bomb, a printer named Cabrinovic, and the Servian student who fired the fatal shots were arrested. They narrowly escaped being lynched by the infuriated crowd.

DUCHESS WHO SHIELDED HUSBAND

Vienna, 28 June – The Archduke Francis Ferdinand, the heir to the Austro-Hungarian throne, and his wife, the Duchess of Hohenberg, were both assassinated today in the street at Sarajevo, the capital of Bosnia.

The Archduke and the Duchess were driving to the town hall when a bomb was thrown at the motor car in which they were seated. The Archduke warded off the bomb with his arm and it fell to the ground, exploding after the car had passed.

Count Boos-Waldeck and First Lieutenant Merrizzi, who were travelling in a car immediately behind the royal car, were slightly wounded and six persons standing at the roadside were also injured.

The bomb-thrower, a printer named Cabrinovic from Trebinje, was arrested.

The Archduke and the Duchess continued their journey to the town hall and on leaving a student from Grahovo named Princip fired several revolver shots at the royal car.

The Archduke was shot in the face and the Duchess in the lower part of the body while she was trying to shield her husband by interposing herself between him and the assassin.

The Archduke and his wife were taken to the Palace, where they died about 11 o'clock.

ASSASSIN NEARLY LYNCHED

Sarajevo (Bosnia), 28 June – As the Archduke Francis Ferdinand and his wife were driving through the streets here today, a young man, stated to be a student, fired revolver shots at their carriage. Both were mortally wounded and succumbed to their injuries in a few minutes.

It appears that two attempts were made on the lives of Archduke Francis Ferdinand and his wife, the Duchess of Hohenberg. The first took place as they were driving to the town hall, when a bomb was thrown at their motor car. This time both the Archduke and his consort escaped unhurt, though several other persons were injured. The perpetrator of the attempt, a compositor of Trebinje, was immediately arrested.

The Archduke and the Duchess resumed their drive to the town hall and during the progress a second attempt was made upon their lives. On this occasion, a high school student fired shots from a Browning pistol, and both the Archduke and the Duchess were fatally wounded and convened to the town hall. Both had meanwhile expired.

Both criminals were almost lynched by the infuriated crowd.

TRAGIC HOUSE OF HAPSBURG

Once again the hand of the assassin plunged the tragic House of Hapsburg into mourning. The Emperor of Austria, whose 84 years of life have been marked by nothing but tragedy, was taking a holiday at Ischl, the first after his serious illness.

The new heir to the throne is the Archduke Karl-Franz Joseph, a popular dashing officer of 27, who married three years ago the beautiful Princess Zita of Bourbon, and who now has a baby boy 18 months old.

The tragic life history of the Emperor Francis Joseph can best be seen in the following:

- ⋆ 1848 – Ascended throne on the abdication of his uncle.
- ⋆ 1865 – His brother, Ludwig Victor, became insane.
- ⋆ 1867 – His brother Maximilian shot in Mexico.
- ⋆ 1868 – Maximilian's wife Charlotte became insane.

★ 1889 – His only son, Archduke Rudolph, either killed or committed suicide.

★ 1898 – His wife, the Empress Elizabeth, assassinated at Genova.

★ 1912 – Archduke Johann Salvator, who married a peasant girl and assumed the name of Johann Orth, went to sea and was never heard of again.

★ 1914 – The heir to the throne and his wife assassinated.

When the news of the assassination of his wife was brought to Emperor Francis Joseph tears came to his eyes, but with a superhuman effort of will power he merely said: "Now I must consecrate my life to work".

So much pain and suffering has been the lot of the aged monarch that, despite this new and additional grief, he will still continue while there is life to work for his peoples.

30 June **1914**

➧ Archduke Francis Ferdinand of Austria was assassinated along with his wife in Sarajevo.

"SOPHIE, LIVE FOR OUR CHILDREN!"

LAST WORDS OF ARCHDUKE TO DYING WIFE

These were the pathetic last words to his wife uttered by the Archduke Francis Ferdinand, heir to the throne of Austria, just before both died together, felled by the assassin's bullets at Sarajevo, the capital of Bosnia.

Nothing in the ghastly tragedy is more poignantly moving than the bereavement of the three children of the Archduke and Duchess – Princess Sophie, who will be 13 next month; Prince Maximilian, aged 11; and Prince Ernest, aged 10.

In one swift blow they are fatherless and motherless, but already the aged Emperor Francis Joseph, despite the shock of such another heavy blow, has given orders that the children are to be in his charge and will live at the palace in Vienna.

His children were always first in the thoughts of the Archduke and, just before leaving Illidze for Sarajevo where he met his death, he sent a telegram to them describing the events of Saturday and concluding with the words: "Greetings and kisses from papa".

It is officially announced that the Kaiser, who was a close friend of the Austrian heir, will go to Vienna to attend the funeral on Saturday. The bodies of the Archduke and the Duchess will be interred in the same grave at the Castle of Artstetten.

Grave disorder in Bosnia has followed the assassinations. Last night it was reported that anti-Servian demonstrations are being made throughout Bosnia, and especially at Sarajevo.

LAST THOUGHT FOR CHILDREN

Sarajevo, 29 June – According to a statement by the Vice-Burgomaster, Herr Vancas, the Duchess, after the first bullet had struck her husband in the throat, threw herself in front of him and embraced him tenderly. Her arms were still clasped round the dying Archduke when a second bullet entered her body.

The assassin, Princip, declared at the judicial examination this morning that he committed the deed out of revenge for the oppression of the Servians. The bombs, which have been discovered, were all manufactured in the Servian Arms Factory.

"I GO WITH THEE"

According to further details received at Vienna, the Archduke was about to drive from the town hall to the hospital to inquire about those of his entourage who had been injured by the bomb, and requested the Duchess not to accompany him but to drive straight back to the Palace.

The Duchess, clinging to her husband, replied: "No, Franz, I go with thee."

SEA ESCORT FOR FUNERAL SHIP

Vienna, 29 June – The bodies of the Archduke Franz Ferdinand and the Duchess of Hohenberg were today taken by train from Sarajevo to Metkovic, in Dalmatia, whence they are to be conveyed by sea under an escort of the Austrian fleet to Trieste. On arrival in Vienna on Friday the bodies will be taken to the Court Chapel where, in the afternoon, a consecration service will be held. In the evening the coffins will be removed to Artstetten.

Vienna, 29 June – The new heir-presumptive, the Archduke Charles Francis, met the Emperor at the railway station this morning and drove him to Schoenbrunn.

It would seem almost a miracle that of the occupants of the motor car which was following that of the Archduke Francis Ferdinand, and under which the bomb exploded, only two persons

were injured. The splinters of the bomb made no fewer than 70 holes in the car.

As the Emperor drove from the station through black-draped streets to Schoenbrunn Castle, the great throngs of people could not, in spite of the seriousness of the occasion, remain from giving his Majesty a stirring ovation, raising loud cheers and waving hats and handkerchiefs.

1 July 1914

BURIAL SHIP'S SOLEMN VOYAGE

TOUCHING TRIBUTE TO AUSTRIA'S GREAT EMPEROR

Our thoughts and hearts turn to the illustrious Sovereign, the Emperor of Austria. He has set an example of patient assiduity and devoted self-sacrifice in pursuit of duty to which there has been no parallel in our own or any other time.

In a fine phrased speech, Mr Asquith paid this tribute to the 70 years' rule of the Emperor Francis Joseph when moving yesterday in the House of Commons a vote of sympathy with Austria on the assassination of the Archduke Francis Ferdinand and his wife.

"One of those inscrutable crimes which almost makes us despair of the progress of mankind," was Mr Asquith's comment.

A resolution tendering to the Austrian Emperor the Commons' "heartfelt and most affectionate sympathy" was carried.

KAISER'S VISIT TO VIENNA

Vienna, 30 June – The Court Chamberlain's department is busily engaged in making preparations for the reception of the bodies of the Archduke and Duchess, which are expected to reach Vienna on Thursday night.

The ceremonies will be held in the chapel of the Imperial Hofburg on Friday. The number of guests will be very limited.

The Emperor William is expected to arrive on Friday. His Majesty will stay only for a few hours, and will return to Berlin after the funeral service.

The Grand Duke Constantine is expected from Russia, the Duke of Aosta from Italy and Prince Arthur of Connaught from England. Other countries are sending special representatives.

TOWN DRAPED IN BLACK

Metkovitch (Dalmatia), 30 June – The special train conveying the bodies of the Archduke and his consort arrived here from Sarajevo this morning.

The town was draped in black, the street lamps were shrouded in crepe, and the flags on the ships in the harbour were all flying at half-mast. A military guard of honour was drawn up on the platform. Those assembled at the station included the schoolchildren with their teachers.

On board the yacht, wreaths were deposited on the two coffins by the Governor and a number of ladies and officers while countless other wreaths covered the vessel.

As the ship slowly got under way the guard of honour fired a general salute.

VILLAGES IN MOURNING

Every little village and hamlet along the River Marenta was draped with mourning, while the whole population of each, including the schoolchildren, was ranged on the banks, headed by the clergy and the communal councils, both men and women bearing lighted candles.

As the naval yacht approached with its sad burden all knelt down, the bells of the village churches tolled and the priests blessed the cortege as it passed.

About nine o'clock the *Viribus Unitis* weighed anchor and, with the war flag and the Archducal standard flying at half-mast, steamed away to the north.

EMPIRE OF MANY NATIONS

One of the most difficult things to understand in connection with Austria-Hungary is the conflict of the large number of races constituting between them the dual monarchy of Austria-Hungary. These races include:

- ⋆ Germans – Their ideals are in the main those of their kinsmen in Germany.
- ⋆ Czechs – Bohemian, with Slav sympathies.
- ⋆ Magyars – Inhabitants of Hungary who have nothing in common with either German or Slav, but in Hungary there is a large population of:
- ⋆ Croats – Slavs who, by race and language but not religion, have much in common with the Servs.
- ⋆ Bosniaks – Inhabitants of Russia and the Herzegovina annexed by Austria, Kinsmen of the Servs.

* Poles – Austria, together with Russia and Germany, carved up Poland but her treatment of the Poles has been good and, although they are Slavs, they are bitterly opposed to Russia.

* Ruthenians – Little Russians from the Ukraine who, on political and religious grounds, hate Russian influence.

6 July **1914**

English soldiers digging a trench prior to the declaration of the First World War.

25 July **1914**

AUSTRIA'S WAR ULTIMATUM

Servia is again the centre of a Balkan problem. As the result of the assassination of the Austrian Archduke Francis Ferdinand and his wife, Austria has presented an ultimatum to Servia. A reply is requested by 6.00pm today.

This ultimatum requests Servia formally condemn the propaganda directed against Austria, to dissolve Pan-Servian societies which are fermenting trouble, and to arrest certain officials alleged to be implicated in the recent crimes at Sarajevo.

Belgrade's reply will be influenced largely by the attitude taken by the Russian Government which, it is stated, will probably urge Servia to make as many concessions as possible in view of the support given by Germany to Austria.

"NO JUSTIFICATION" NEEDED

Budapest, 24 July – At the opening of the sitting in the Lower House of the Hungarian Parliament today the Prime Minister rose at once and informed the House that the Austro-Hungarian Minister yesterday communicated the Note to the Servian Government, and that at the same time the Note was sent to the Ambassadors accredited to the signatory Powers. The Prime Minister added:

"The step taken requires no justification. We ought rather to explain why we have only just taken it.

"We wanted to wait until the investigations at Sarajevo had thrown complete light on certain circumstances.

"We also wanted to avoid any appearance of being guided by passion or righteous indignation. The step was indeed taken after the most mature consideration.

"It is by no means aggressive nor does it imply any provocation, as we demand nothing else in the Note than what Servia must conceive her natural and neighbourly duty.

"No one can reproach us with seeking war. We have rather gone to the utmost limit of our patience."

Count Andrassy, on behalf of all the opposition, declared that Servia's hatred for the monarchy had grown in proportion with her successes in territorial extension.

The President said that if the business of the day was disposed of the sitting would be closed and Parliament would not meet again until Tuesday.

Vienna, 24 July – It is expected here that, in spite of the categorical tone and far-reaching nature of Austria-Hungary's demands, Servia will not give in. No negotiations and no bargaining will, it is understood, be allowed.

Should Servia's reply be a negative one, it is reported here that the army will be called upon to enforce the Austrian demands.

AUSTRIA'S FATEFUL NOTE

Vienna, 23 July – At six o'clock this evening the Austro-Hungarian Minister in Belgrade presented to the Servian Government a verbal Note containing the demands of the Monarchy with regard to the suppression of the Pan-Servian movement and the punishment of those concerned in the Sarajevo assassinations. A reply is required by six o'clock on Saturday evening. The Note says:

"The history of recent years, and in particular the painful events of 28 June last, have shown the existence in Servia of a subversive movement with the object of detaching a part of Austria-Hungary from the Monarchy.

"The Royal Servian Government . . . has permitted the criminal machinations of various societies and associations and has tolerated unrestrained language on the part of the Press apologies for the perpetrators of the outrages.

"In short, it has permitted all the manifestations which have incited the Servian population to hatred of the Monarchy and contempt of its institutions."

27 July **1914**

CRISIS THAT THREATENS THE FUTURE OF THE WHOLE OF EUROPE

AUSTRIA BREAKS OFF RELATIONS WITH SERVIA

Vienna, Sunday night – M Jovanovitch, the Servian Minister in Vienna, has been sent his passports. This is generally taken to be an equivalent of a declaration of war.

Europe is face to face with the greatest crisis of modern times. It is of such momentous gravity that, if the worst comes to the worst, it would be a war that would alter the face of Europe.

The crucial point is – will Great Britain be involved?

So far there is no confirmation of the rumour that Austria-Hungary has actually declared war on Servia.

There was a Central News Vienne message last night to the effect that it was rumoured at Zemlin that first shots had been fired between Austrians and Servians near Semendria.

Servia's reply to Austria's ten-pointed Note was found to be unsatisfactory on Saturday, and the Austrian Minister left Belgrade.

Diplomatic relations have been broken off, and the next step, unless diplomacy averts it, is war.

The text of the Servian reply to Austria, published yesterday, says a Paris Reuter telegram, shows that the Servian Government accepts all the conditions asked for by Austria-Hungary with the exception of one demanding the co-operation of Austro-Hungarian officials in Servia itself in the suppression of anti-Austria propaganda. It does not, however, give a formal refusal to this.

Finally, the reply states that if the Austro-Hungarian Government found these explanations insufficient the Servian Government appealed to The Hague Tribunal and to the various Powers who signed the declaration of 1909 regarding Bosnia and Herzegovina.

A late Central News message stated that a general mobilisation has been ordered in Montenegro.

The King, according to present arrangements, will abandon his visit to Goodwood.

It was originally intended that his Majesty should leave town today, but in view of the international crisis and affairs in Ireland his Majesty has decided to remain at Buckingham Palace, so as to keep in close touch with his Ministers.

Prince Henry of Prussia, brother of the German Emperor, visited the King yesterday.

AUSTRIANS FIRED ON?

Vienna, 26 July – Advices from Semlin state that rumours are current there, according to which the first encounter between Austrians and Servians has taken place near Kevevara, close to Semendria.

It is stated that Danube tug boats which are conveying a company of Austrian infantry were fired on from the Servian shore.

They returned the fire, and more than a hundred shots were exchanged. Further details are lacking.

The Austrian authorities have seized two ships at Kubin which refused to stop when called upon, and further fired upon Austrian soldiers.

THE KING'S REPORTED ACTION

Paris newspapers, says the Central News, publish telegrams from St Petersburg, according to which King George has addressed a letter to the German Emperor counselling the maintenance of the peace of Europe.

AUSTRIA-HUNGARY

HANDED HIS PASSPORTS

Vienna, 26 July – M Jovanovitch, the Servian Minister, was informed this morning of the rupture of diplomatic relations between Austria-Hungary and Servia, and was at the same time handed his passports. He afterwards visited the Russian Charge d'Affaires.

While travelling from Gleishenberg to Belgrade, General Putnik, Servian Chief of Staff, was arrested on Saturday night by the Austrian military authorities, but was later released.

RUSSIA

RUSSIANS LOOKING TO ENGLAND

St Petersburg, 26 July – Not a voice is raised here against Russia giving her support to Servia. The *Novoye Vremya* says: "All eyes here are turned upon England; who is regarded as occupying an exclusive position in the destinies of Europe."

Paris, 26 July – A special telegram from St Petersburg to the *Excelsior* dated 11.45 last night states that at a meeting of the council of Ministers held this afternoon, after a very strong appeal from the War Minister, the immediate mobilisation of the army corps of Odessa and Kieff was decided upon.

At the same meeting the Tsar signed a decree naming the Grand Duke Nicholas Micolawitz generalissimo of the army.

St Petersburg, 26 July – A scene of much enthusiasm witnessed at Krasnoe Selo when the Tsar addressed the cadets who have been unexpectedly commissioned and are joining their regiments at once.

SERVIA

KING PETER LEAVES BELGRADE

Vienna, 25 July – The Court, the Government and the garrison are leaving Belgrade. The administration will be conducted from Kragujevacs, which is a strong strategic position.

The Servian Legation in London yesterday received a telegram from Kragujevacs, stating that the Crown Prince had ordered a general mobilisation, and that the Skupstina had been summoned to meet at Nish today.

ITALY

"A FRIENDLY ATTITUDE"

Vienna, 26 July – It is officially announced that the Italian Government has informed the Austro-Hungarian Government that in the event of an armed conflict between Austria-Hungary and Servia it will adopt a friendly attitude in accordance with the relations of the Alliance.

BELGIUM

READY TO ARM

Brussels, 26 July – The Ministry of War is preparing for the reinforcement of the peace effectives, and all plans have been completed for a general mobilisation. The *Soir* says that Belgium is watching events and will do her duty.

GERMANY

KAISER'S SUDDEN RETURN

Bergen (Norway), 26 July – The Emperor William left here suddenly at 6.00pm for Germany. It is stated that all the divisions of the German fleet got orders to gather tonight at pre-arranged places off the Norwegian coast.

Berlin, 26 July – Denial is given to the report that the German fleet is concentrating off the Scandinavian coast. The chief of the German Army, Von Moltke, has been called back from Carlsbad to Berlin.

GREAT BRITAIN

DIPLOMATIC CALLS IN LONDON

Sir Arthur Nicholson, Permanent Under-Secretary at the Foreign Office, called at the Austrian and Russian Embassies yesterday. Both Sir Edward Grey and Mr Asquith are out of town, but kept closely in touch with affairs. The German Ambassador called at the Foreign Office yesterday.

FRANCE

NIGHT CONFERENCE IN PARIS

Paris, 26 July – The German Ambassador in Paris paid a long visit today to the Quai d'Orsay. There is no excitement on the boulevards. It is stated that Servia's answer to the Austrian Note was in the nature of a request that Austria should more fully explain the nature of her demands, while she protested against the proposal to establish an Austro-Hungarian police in Servia.

Paris, 26 July – M Messimy, the War Minister, conferred throughout the night with the chiefs of the army, and the Midi is in a position to state that important steps were taken. All the officers and chiefs of staff who were on holiday have been telegraphically recalled to their various posts. Prefects and sous-prefects have also been ordered to return.

IS GREAT BRITAIN FREE?

Now that Austria is on the point of declaring war the question that everyone is asking in this country is: "Are we likely to be involved?"

No definite answer to this can be given, but the probabilities are that eventually if Europe were turned into a cockpit that we also would have to take our share of fighting.

Austria has always been alarmed and more than a little jealous of Servia's rise. She has perpetually belittled her neighbour, and whenever possible tried to stop her trade.

A glance at the map will show how easy this was. Servia's only outlet to the world at large is by way of the Danube, and Austria commands that and the Servian capital by the guns of Zemlin.

On the other hand, Austria feels that Servia has been disloyal to her promises and that Servia has actively encouraged groups of murderers, and that these encouragements eventually ended in the assassination of the Archduke Francis Ferdinand and his Consort.

If war were confined to Austria and Servia nobody in this country, at any rate, would care very much what happened.

IF RUSSIA STARTS

There are, however, other points to remember. The first is that Russia is the guardian angel of the Slavs throughout the world.

If Russia starts fighting then Germany has got to join in for, quite apart from the Triple Alliance, Germany and Austria entered into what was called by diplomats "the Russian Insurance Policy", by which either country is automatically bound to go to the support of the other in case of attack by Russia.

We thus already have Austria, Servia, Russia and Germany engaged. France is bound to Russia by an alliance only strengthened and reaffirmed last week.

Are we likely to be involved in the war?

Common sense will tell us no. It is generally understood from Sir Edward Grey's repeated assurances that we are not in any way bound to Russia, but it is certainly an open question whether or not we would be compelled to go to the aid of France.

R, JULY 27, 1914 Page 3

SHALL A SPARK FROM A MURDERER'S PISTOL SET ALL EUROPE IN A BLAZE?

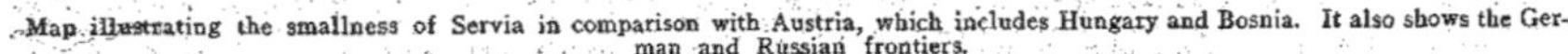
Map illustrating the smallness of Servia in comparison with Austria, which includes Hungary and Bosnia. It also shows the German and Russian frontiers.

General Putnik, the chief of the Servian General Staff, who will be in charge of Servia's army.

r. von Bethmann-Hollweg, German Chancellor.

M. Sazonoff, Russia's Foreign Minister.

The murdered Duchess.

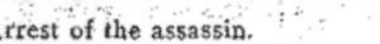
Arrest of the assassin.

The Archduke Ferdinand.

Count Berchtold, Servia's Foreign Minister.

M. Pasitch, Servian Prime Minister.

Although the situation between Austria and Servia has for long been strained, the terrible assassination of the Archduke Ferdinand and his wife, the Duchess of Hohenburg, at Serajevo seems likely to be the spark that will light the fires of war between the two countries and possibly set all Europe blazing in the most terrible conflict of modern times. Already war fever has broken out in the capitals of Europe, and Russia is actually mobilising troops. What will Germany do?

The First Declarations of War

28 July **1914** – 3 August **1914**

Austria-Hungary failed to get the satisfactory response from Servia and so declared war. The fact that Russia – perhaps feeling somewhat guilty she hadn't provided more backing for her neighbour in recent years – ordered a full mobilisation that resulted in a declaration of war by Germany. The cogs had begun to engage in a way that was impossible to stop.

As soon as war broke out, men began volunteering for the armed forces in unprecedented numbers. These recruits are being trained on how to manoeuvre large artillery pieces by Territorial Army instructors, August 1914.

28 July **1914**

CAN SIR E GREY STOP GENERAL WAR?

FRANCE AND ITALY ACCEPT PLAN FOR LONDON CONFERENCE – AUSTRIA ABOUT TO ATTACK?

Has Sir Edward Grey saved Europe from a general war? It was on him that all eyes were turned yesterday when every nation concerned in the Austro-Servian dispute stood alert ready to spring to arms.

He announced in the House of Commons yesterday that he was engaged in an attempt to arrange a conference between the French, German and Italian Ambassadors in London to try to arrange a settlement.

"It must be obvious to anyone who reflects," he said, "that the moment the dispute ceases to be one between Austria and Servia it can but end in the gravest catastrophe which has fallen upon the Concert of Europe at one blow.

"No one can see what issues would be raised, and the consequences thereof, direct and indirect, would be incalculable."

France and Italy, it is announced, have accepted Sir E Grey's mediation proposal, and a calmer feeling was reported from Germany and Russia.

Austria, however, continues to act as if war were inevitable, and preparations for hostilities are being made in every state.

The British fleet is ready for action, and leave to officers and men has been stopped.

READY TO ATTACK TODAY

Paris, 28 July (12.50am) – It is confirmed here by messages from Vienna that Austria has completed final preparations to attack Servia this morning.

REPORTED INVASION OF SERVIA

A telegram to the Berlin *Lokal-Anzeiger* from Vienna says that the Austrian Army has invaded Servia at Mitrovitza, about 50 miles west of Belgrade, in accordance with the Vienna General Staff's plan of campaign, driving the Servian troops before them.

The Austrian Danube flotilla is stated to have captured two Servian steamers, taking some of the enemy prisoners.

AUSTRIAN TROOPS FIRED ON

Vienna, 27 July – Servian troops on a Danube steamer near Temes-Kubin (Hungary) have fired on Austro-Hungarian troops, who returned fire. An engagement of some importance ensued.

Berlin, 27 July – The papers publish telegrams from Vienna, according to which the Servians have blown up the bridge over the Danube.

RUSSIANS MOVE ON FRONTIER

Berlin, 27 July – The *Eydtkuhnen Zeitung* states that the frontier watch reports large movements of troops at Wirballen, in Russian Poland.

Copenhagen, 27 July – According to private advices from St Petersburg, several Russian harbours on the Baltic, including Dunamunde, near Riga, have been closed by mines.

Vienna, 27 July – It is announced that as from 27 July the Orient Express trains will start from Budapest and terminate their journey there respectively. The Orient Express normally runs through to Constantinople.

BRITISH FLEET READY

The British First Fleet was busily engaged in coaling at Portland yesterday, preparatory to taking a cruise to sea, to a destination which is understood to be somewhere in the North Sea, near Hull or Harwich. It has been decided not to reopen the schools after the manoeuvres for the present; consequently the balance of crews of the Second Fleet ships and vessels will remain in their ships.

Gibraltar, 27 July – All furlough has been cancelled. Officers who were leaving for home today have returned to duty. The battleship *Bellerophon*, which is due tomorrow for a refit, will await orders instead of going into dockyard hands.

RULERS HURRY HOME

The Hague, 27 July – Queen Wilhelmina arrived this morning unexpectedly. She will remain here a few days on account of the foreign situation. President Poincaré is hurrying back to France from Scandinavian waters as fast as the warship *Franc* can carry him. He has cancelled his visits to Copenhagen and Christiania.

THE DAILY MIRROR. Wednesday, July 29, 1914.

AUSTRIA DECLARES WAR ON SERVIA.

The Daily Mirror

LATEST CERTIFIED CIRCULATION MORE THAN 1,000,000 COPIES PER DAY

No. 3,358. Registered at the G.P.O. as a Newspaper. WEDNESDAY, JULY 29, 1914 One Halfpenny.

AUSTRIA-HUNGARY DECLARES WAR ON SERVIA: ARE WE ON THE EVE OF A TERRIBLE EUROPEAN CONFLICT?

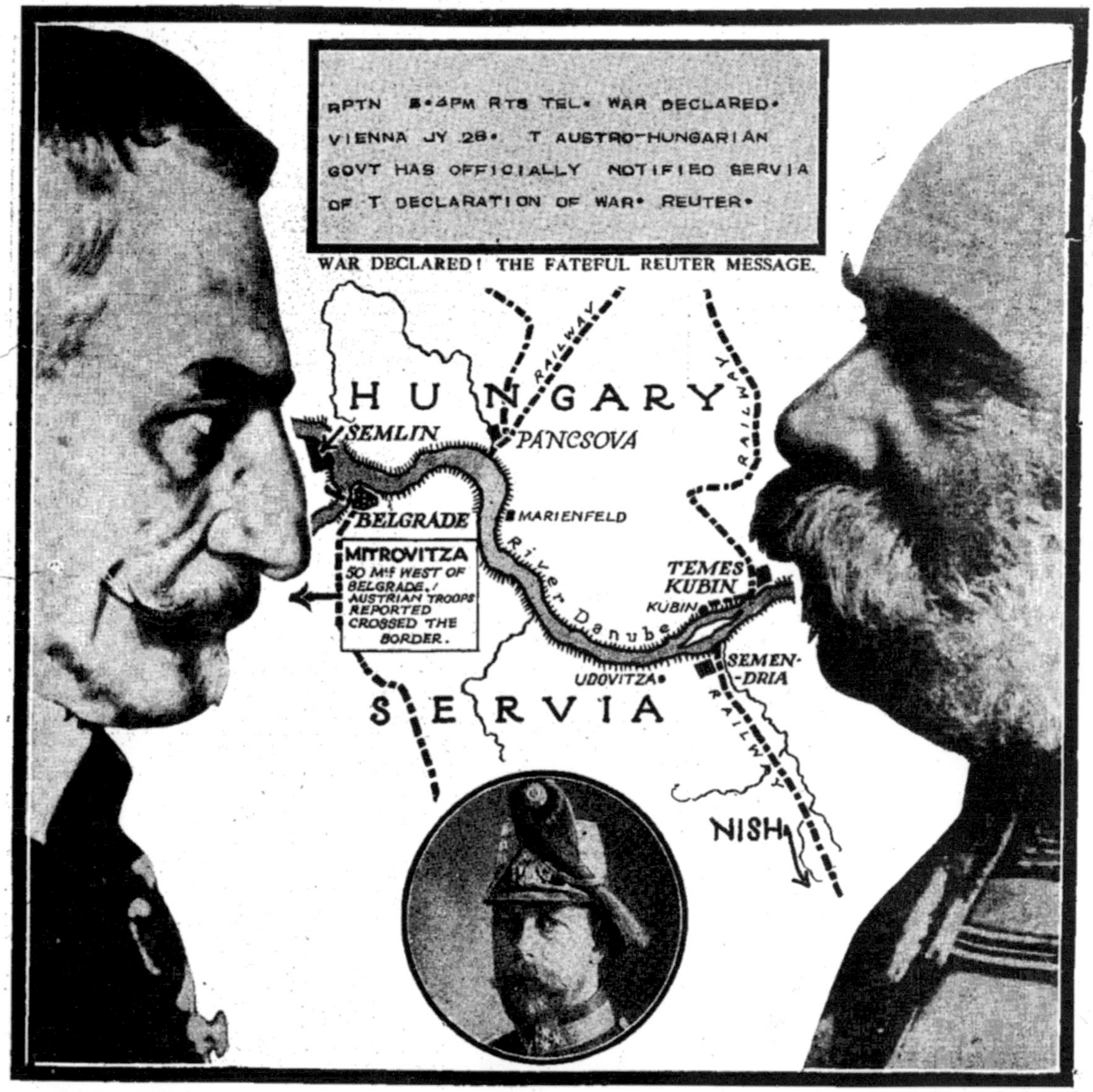

RPTN 5.4PM RTS TEL. WAR DECLARED. VIENNA JY 28. T AUSTRO-HUNGARIAN GOVT HAS OFFICIALLY NOTIFIED SERVIA OF T DECLARATION OF WAR. REUTER.

WAR DECLARED! THE FATEFUL REUTER MESSAGE.

HUNGARY
SEMLIN
PANCSOVA
RAILWAY
BELGRADE
MARIENFELD
MITROVITZA 50 MS WEST OF BELGRADE. AUSTRIAN TROOPS REPORTED CROSSED THE BORDER.
River Danube
TEMES KUBIN
KUBIN
SEMENDRIA
UDOVITZA
SERVIA
NISH

King Peter of Servia. How the River Danube— King George as Austrian colonel. —divides the two countries. The Emperor Francis Joseph.

The war cloud which has been hanging over Europe has burst, and "Austria-Hungary find ... safe... its rights and interests and to have recourse for this ... of the news cannot easily be exaggerated, ... most terrible co... modern times. The whole Continent is, indeed, preparing for the worst, and mobilisation is going on everywhere. The most interesting figure at the moment is Austria's aged Emperor, the murder of whose heir is the immediate cause of the war. King Peter abdicated quite recently, and the Regent is Prince Alexandre.

These crowds at the Oxford v Cambridge Varsity cricket match at Lord's in July 1914 were blissfully unaware of the turmoil about to be unleashed on the world.

Berlin, 27 July – The Emperor arrived at Wildpark Station this afternoon.

HELP FROM FAR AWAY

Pekin, 27 July – The Austrian Minister at Pekin has issued a proclamation ordering Austrian reservists to return to Europe.

NEW TROUBLE FOR SERVIA

Salonika, 27 July – In view of the departure of the bulk of Servia's troops from New Servia to the Austro-Hungarian frontier, Bulgarian bands are reported to be preparing to invade Servian territory in the Strumnitza region.

PREPARING NOT TO FIGHT

Amsterdam, 27 July – The Dutch Government is preparing to take measures for the maintenance of neutrality in the event of a war in Eastern Europe. There is great activity in the departments of war and marine.

LONDON'S CONTINGENT OF AUSTRIANS

Between 500 and 600 Austrians and Hungarians in England are liable to be called to rejoin the colours. The offices of the Consul-General were besieged yesterday with men expressing their readiness to go.

29 July **1914**

THE TERRIBLE DANGER THAT THREATENS EUROPE

Russia has declared she will not see Servia crushed. Relations between her and Austria are dangerously strained, and Russian troops are being hurried to the frontier.

Germany has rejected the English proposal for a peace conference, and will support Austria if Russia attacks her.

France is bound by a strict alliance to join forces with Russia in any war in Europe.

Italy is allied to Germany and Austria. Though not in reality friendly to Austria, she has engaged to support her in a European conflict. Italy is friendly to Britain.

Britain is joined by close ties, though not by a formal alliance, to France and Russia who count on her backing. Britain is bound to declare the neutrality of Belgium if her territory is invaded during a Franco-German war.

The danger to Europe is that:

* Russia will defend the Servians by force of arms.

* Germany would then join the war.

* France would have to take the side of Russia and Italy that of Austria and Germany.

* Britain may thus be involved.

There is also a possibility that the Balkan States – Rumania, Greece and Bulgaria – with Turkey, may join in the war.

DECLARATION OF WAR BY AUSTRIA-HUNGARY ON SERVIA

EUROPE IN ARMS

The Austro-Hungarian Government has officially notified Servia of the declaration of war. This was the fateful message received in London from Reuter's Vienna correspondent at 5.30pm yesterday.

The war is the outcome of Servia's refusal to allow Austria to supervise the investigation in Servia into the murder of the Archduke Franz Ferdinand and his wife at Sarajevo by a Servian sympathiser. Austria in her ultimatum required many other concessions which Servia granted. The Servian reply was considered by Austria to be "filled with the spirit of dishonesty", and yesterday's declaration was the dread sequel.

TEXT OF THE FORMAL DECLARATION

Vienna, 28 July – The formal declaration of war was published in a special edition of the *Official Gazette*. It is worded as follows:

"The Royal Government of Servia, not having given a satisfactory reply to the Note presented to it by the Austro-Hungarian Minister in Belgrade on 24 July 1914, the Imperial and Royal Government of Austria-Hungary finds itself necessary to safeguard its rights and interests, and to have recourse for this purpose to force of arms.

"Austria-Hungary therefore considers itself from this moment in a state of war with Servia.

"Signed Count Berchtold, Austro-Hungarian Minister for Foreign Affairs."

AUSTRIANS CROSS FRONTIER

Berlin, 28 July – A telegram from Vienna to the *Lokal-Anzeiger* states that Austrian troops have crossed the Servo-Hungarian frontier and are continuing their march on Mitrovitza. The Servians have been driven back.

Paris, 28 July – The *Militaerische Rundschau* asserts that a Servian division newly formed in the Sanjak is pushing strong detachments towards Priboj, including many volunteer organisations, is noticeable near Drin on the frontier. The Montenegrin troops near Plevlje are in close contact with the Servian troops near Priboj.

SERVIAN STEAMER CAPTURED

Nish (by indirect route), 27 July – The Servian steamer *Deligrad* was taken possession of at Orchava by the Austrians, and the passengers on board were detained. The Austrians at once hauled down the Servian colours and replaced them with their own.

An Austrian tug, which had already in tow the Servian steamer *Morava* as well as several barges, likewise took the *Deligrad* in tow.

AUSTRIA'S ARMY

On the war footing Austria-Hungary can dispose of about 2,500,000 trained men, with some 8,500 guns. Strenuous efforts have been made in the last two years to improve the mobilisation and organisation of the army, but it has two serious defects:

* A large number of the soldiers are Slavs and as such may be prone to sympathise with Servia.

* In time of peace the number of men with the colours has until recent years been too small to permit a thorough training of the reservists.

SERVIA'S ARMY

The Servian Army on the eve of war was in process of reorganisation. The rifle is the Mauser of .27 calibre; the field gun a French Creusot quick-firer of pattern similar to that employed in the French Army and three-inch calibre.

ZEPPELIN V SENT TO FRONTIER

The Kaiser was in conference throughout yesterday with his political, military and naval chiefs. The opinion prevails in Potsdam that the mobilisation of the German Army and war are imminent.

The war spirit in Berlin has cooled off as far as "demonstrations" are concerned. The police today decided to prohibit further processions through the streets on the ground that they interfere with traffic.

The military airship *Zeppelin V* was transferred yesterday from Johannisthal to Posen, near the Russian frontier.

AUSTRIA NEGOTIATING WITH RUSSIA TO AVERT GENERAL WAR

GERMANY REJECTS PROPOSAL OF CONFERENCE – WHAT IS EUROPE DOING?

Feeling in the capitals:

* St Petersburg – Excited, cheering crowds.

* Berlin – Situation judged gloomily.

* Rome – Quiet. Talk in favour of neutrality.

* Paris – Calm. Reservists buying uniforms.

Can Europe still escape a general war?

Is Britain to be dragged into a stupendous conflict simply because Austrians and Servians have quarelled?

Sir Edward Grey's great effort to avert it by calling a peace conference has failed. Germany rejected his proposal, courteously but firmly. One gleam of hope still remains – Austria has entered, it is said, into direct negotiations with Russia.

If the latter country can be persuaded not to enter actively into the conflict, it is still possible that Europe may be saved from the last catastrophe of a huge international war.

Meanwhile every European nation, great or small, is preparing for the worst. Armies and fleets are being concentrated at strategic points; special troop trains are in readiness to start at any moment on every frontier.

WHY GERMANY SAID "NO"

Berlin, 28 July – It is officially announced that the German Government has rejected the British proposals for a conference.

"Despite our sympathy with Sir Edward Grey's efforts for the preservation of peace, we are unable to see that his idea of a conference in London offers any prospect of finding a way out of the difficulty.

"Austria cannot consent to appear before a European tribunal like a Balkan State and explain her actions and allow her policy to be influenced by the decisions of such a court."

ORDERS TO GERMAN FLEET

Berlin, 28 July – It is officially announced that the German fleet is returning to home waters, and concentrating at Wilhelmshaven and Kiel.

RUSSIAN TROOPS ON FRONTIER

Berlin, 28 July – Russian troops – cavalry, pioneers, artillery and two regiments of infantry – are reported to have occupied the Russian frontier railway station at Wirballen.

A squadron of German Uhlans has been sent from Stellupoenen to the German frontier railway station at Eydtkuhnen.

COAST LIGHTS PUT OUT

St Petersburg, 28 July – The *Official Gazette* publishes an order prohibiting merchant and private ships from passing between Helsingfors and Hangoe.

The floating lighthouse at Eraugsgrund has been removed. The Grohara light and other lights off Helsingfors have been extinguished.

GERMANY READY TO COUNTER

Berlin, 28 July – It is intimated in well-informed quarters that even a partial mobilisation by Russia as a reply to the Austrian declaration of war on Servia would cause an immediate mobilisation by Germany which nothing could then hold back.

FRENCH TROOPS CONCENTRATING

Belfort, 28 July – The concentration of the troops of the 7th Army Corps is being hastened. Numerous military trains are arriving at Belfort and neighbouring towns.

ITALIAN WARSHIPS RECALLED

Three Italian warships with several hundred officers and cadets have been recalled from the Clyde.

BELGIAN SOLDIERS RECALLED

Brussels, 28 July – It is announced that soldiers on leave are to return to their regiments tonight.

BRITAIN READY

FLEETS PREPARED FOR INSTANT ACTION – FLOTILLA SENT TO EAST COAST

The British First Battle Fleet – the most powerful in the world – is ready at Portland for immediate action. Leave granted yesterday evening to First Fleet men was suddenly stopped at eight o'clock and the men were ordered to go aboard at once. Masters-at-arms and police went out to search all theatres and other places of amusement where sailors were likely to be found.

The Second Fleet can be put in striking position within 24 hours. The Third Fleet could be ready with full compliments aboard in 48 hours. It would be unusually efficient, as the reserves of which its crews are mainly composed have only just finished 10 days' training.

Mobilisation was proceeding at Portsmouth yesterday. All the men have been recalled to barracks, and ready to go on board at once.

The destroyer flotilla is under orders to be in readiness for an immediate call.

A special train from Portsmouth arrived at Dover yesterday with seamen to complete the warships to full crews. All leave has been stopped in the flotilla.

30 July **1914**

"TO MY PEOPLE!" – EMPEROR'S WAR MANIFESTO

On the outbreak of war with Servia the aged Austrian Emperor has issued a stirring appeal to his subjects. Francis Joseph says:

"It was my fervent wish to consecrate the years which by the grace of God still remain to me to the works of peace and to protect my peoples from the heavy sacrifices and burdens of war. Providence in its wisdom has otherwise decreed.

"With a quickly forgetful ingratitude, the Kingdom of Servia, which from the first beginnings of its independence as a State until quite recently had been supported and assisted by my ancestors, has for years trodden the path of open hostility to Austria-Hungary.

"The flame of its hatred for myself and my house has blazed always higher; the design to tear from us by force inseparable portions of Austria-Hungary has been made manifest with less and less disguise.

"A series of murderous attacks, an organised, carefully prepared and well carried out conspiracy, whose fruitful success wounded me and my loyal peoples to the heart, forms a visible bloody track of those secret machinations which were operated and directed in Servia.

"A halt must be called to these intolerable proceedings, and an end must be put to incessant provocations of Servia.

"In this solemn hour I am fully conscious of the whole

THE DAILY MIRROR, Thursday, July 30, 1914.

IMPORTANT TRADE NOTICE. *Please order extra copies of Monday's "Daily Mirror" Grand Holiday Number. THERE WILL BE A RECORD DEMAND.*

The Daily Mirror

LATEST CERTIFIED CIRCULATION MORE THAN 1,000,000 COPIES PER DAY

No. 3,359. Registered at the G.P.O. as a Newspaper. THURSDAY, JULY 30, 1914 One Halfpenny.

WILL GERMANY FIGHT SIDE BY SIDE WITH AUSTRIA? AN EXCITED POPULACE CLAMOURS FOR WAR, BUT DRAWS ITS MONEY FROM THE BANKS.

Bavaria wants war, and clamours for it at a great mass meeting.

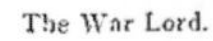

The War Lord.

Police keep back the crowd which besieged a Berlin savings bank.

Customers demolish a Munich café because patriotic songs were forbidden.

Germany, that is, the ordinary man in the street, is in a bellicose mood. Nothing but war, it would appear, will satisfy the people, who are demanding vengeance on Servia at mass meetings all over the country. Their temper may be judged from the fact that a café at Munich was wrecked because the landlord, noticing some Servians among his customers, declined to allow the band to play patriotic songs. Meanwhile, there is a run on the savings banks, which are besieged by depositors.

significance of my resolve and any responsibility before the Almighty. I have examined and weighed everything, and with a serene conscience I set out on the path to which my duty points.

"I trust in my peoples, who throughout every storm have always rallied in unity and loyalty around my throne, and have always been prepared for the severest sacrifices for the honour, the greatness and the might of the Fatherland.

"I trust in Austria-Hungary's brave and devoted forces, and I trust in the Almighty to give the victory to my arms."

FIGHTING BEGINS AT BELGRADE

Fighting has swiftly followed Austria's declaration of war. On the Servians blowing up the bridge between Belgrade and Semlin, the Austrians delivered an attack by artillery and their small warships on the Danube on the Servian positions, from which the Servians withdrew.

The Kaiser has held a War Council on learning of the partial mobilisation of the Russian Army, and German troops are moving to the frontier.

These were the outstanding features of a situation that grew rapidly worse last night.

War fever is raging in St Petersburg and Vienna, and Berlin has grown pessimistic.

"The English Government," Mr Asquith said in the House of Commons yesterday, "are not relaxing their efforts to circumscribe the area of the conflict. The situation at the moment is one of extreme gravity."

"BELGRADE BOMBARDED"

Paris, 29 July – It is confirmed here from Vienna that Belgrade has been bombarded by the Austrians. The Servians dynamited a bridge over the Save, and were fired upon by the Austrians, whereupon they retired to Belgrade. The Save is a tributary of the Danube, which it joins a few miles from Belgrade.

FIRST FIGHTING

Vienna, 29 July – A semi-official communication issued here says:

"At 1.30 this morning the Servians blew up the bridge between Semlin and Belgrade.

"Our infantry and artillery, in co-operation with the monitors on the Danube, fired on the Servian positions on the further side of the river.

"The Servians withdrew after a brief engagement.

"Our losses were quite insignificant.

"Yesterday a small detachment of pioneers, in co-operation with the Customs officers, succeeded in capturing two Servian steamers laden with ammunition and mines.

"The pioneers and the revenue guards, after a short but sharp encounter, overcame the Servian crews of the ships, although the latter were superior in numbers, and took possession of their vessels and their dangerous cargo, which were towed away by two of our Danube steamers."

KAISER'S GRAVE STEP

Berlin, 29 July – Upon the news reaching here that Russia had decided upon a partial mobilisation, a conference was immediately called by the Kaiser, who summoned the Imperial Chancellor, the Ministers of War and Marine, the chiefs of the army and naval staffs and the Foreign Secretary.

It is understood that in official circles, the chances of the war being localised are regarded as less favourable. The outlook is pessimistic.

GERMAN FRONTIER ACTIVITY

Berlin, 29 July – There are abundant signs that Russia is taking comprehensive military precautions on the German frontier, to which the Germans are naturally replying.

Messages from Eydtkuhnen, the first railway station on the German side of the frontier, state that there is a large force of Russian troops at Kibarty, a stone's throw from the frontier.

On the German side, it is reported that three regiments have been brought to full war strength, while last night a regiment of infantry was sent to Absteinen, and two regiments to Stallupoenen, close to Eydtkuhnen.

"SITUATION NOT IMPROVED"

Berlin, 29 July – The *Vossiche Zeitung*, in an evening edition, advances the opinion that the situation has not been improved by the fact that Russia, while negotiating diplomatically, continues the movement of troops. The paper thinks that this diminishes the chance of the war being localised.

TSAR ON "SERIOUS EVENTS"

St Petersburg, 29 July – The cadets at the naval school were today promoted to the rank of officers in the presence of the Tsar, who said: "I have given orders that you should be incorporated in the army in view of the serious events through which Russia is at present passing."

THE DAILY MIRROR, Friday, July 31, 1914.

IMPORTANT TRADE NOTICE. *You will need extra copies of Monday's "Daily Mirror" Grand Holiday Number. THERE WILL BE A RECORD DEMAND.*

The Daily Mirror

LATEST CERTIFIED CIRCULATION MORE THAN 1,000,000 COPIES PER DAY

No. 3,360. Registered at the G.P.O. as a Newspaper. FRIDAY, JULY 31, 1914 One Halfpenny.

WAR OFFICE "PRECAUTIONS": TROOPS GUARD WOOLWICH ARSENAL, TILBURY DOCKS AND THE GOVERNMENT GUNPOWDER FACTORY.

Armed sentry on duty at Tilbury Docks.

The entrance to the docks guarded by a machine gun.

Waiting their turn for duty at Woolwich.

A sentry near the Arsenal.

According to a statement issued by the War Office yesterday the only orders that have been given in connection with the European crisis are "purely precautionary and of a defensive character." Nevertheless, these precautionary measures are being taken on a pretty wide scale. Troops are moving in various parts of the country, police leave has been stopped, and soldiers are guarding Woolwich Arsenal, the small arms factory at Enfield Lock, the gunpowder factory at Waltham Abbey and the Tilbury Docks. Two guns have also been mounted on the towers at Purfleet for dealing, it is believed, with hostile aircraft.—(*Daily Mirror* and L.N.A.)

ONLY A MIRACLE CAN AVERT A WAR

St Petersburg, 29 July – In Russian eyes, the die is cast, and only a political miracle can avert war. A partial mobilisation has already been ordered and there is every indication that the whole of the vast military machinery will soon be set in motion.

HOW RUSSIA IS MOBILISING

It is stated that the Russian mobilisation is confined to military districts of Kieff, Odessa, Moscow and Kazan. In each district are four army corps on a peace footing. Mobilisation converts the 16 army corps into 32. The mobilisation affects the Austrian and not the German frontier.

WAR FEVER IN ST PETERSBURG

St Petersburg, 29 July – A crowd of 20,000 persons of all classes gave a vociferous farewell at the station tonight to a few Servian reserve officers who were leaving to join the colours. Popular feeling is hourly becoming more intense. At two o'clock this afternoon great patriotic demonstrations began on the Nevsky Prospekt. At five o'clock the demonstrations were still in progress, and were renewed with vigour.

BRITISH FLEET SAILS

The First Fleet, under the orders of Admiral Sir G Callaghan, left Portland yesterday with sealed orders. The bands of all the ships played, as they went out. As each ship passed the entrance the crew broke into cheers. When outside the harbour the fleet formed up and was rapidly lost to view.

Malta, 29 July – The Mediterranean Fleet is expected here tomorrow afternoon at one o'clock. Preparations are actively proceeding for the fleet to take in coal, ammunition and provisions immediately after its arrival.

NO BRITISH MOBILISATION

The following communiqué was issued by the War Office last night:

"No measures have been taken by the military authorities which are of the nature of mobilisation.

"The only orders that have been given are purely precautionary and of a defensive character. The naval measures are also precautionary, and no mobilisation has been ordered."

VIENNA'S WAR ENTHUSIASM

Vienna, 29 July – Popular enthusiasm since the declaration of war and the issue of the Emperor's manifesto has been constantly growing. Crowds are everywhere gathering in the streets, cheering the soldiers and singing the national anthem. Troops leaving for the front are given great ovations.

GERMAN FLEETS RETURNING

Berlin, 29 July – It is announced that the ships of the North Sea Fleet returned to Wilhelmshaven yesterday evening, and those of the Baltic Fleet to Kiel this morning.

SERVIAN AIRMEN ACTIVE

Vienna, 29 July – The Servian movements of troops, so far as they are reported, have as their objective points Valjevo (47 miles south-west of Belgrade), Azice and Svilajnac (to the north-west of Nish).

Strong divisions of volunteers, with some regulars, are reported along the Drina line near Leschnic (on the Servian-Bosnian frontier, near the junction of the Drina with the Danube).

A Montenegrin brigade with mountain artillery is near Priboj (near the Montenegrin-Servian frontier).

Montenegrin women are reported to be assisting in the building or earthworks at certain points which are kept secret.

Servian troops which were posted on the Bulgarian border have been transported northward. Servian airmen are flying along the border. News received from several points in Montenegro's recently acquired territory report disorders and disaffection among the populace, which is opposed to the war.

31 July **1914**

BRITAIN SHOWS UNITED FRONT IN WAR PERIL

GERMAN DEMAND TO RUSSIA

While Europe was waiting in doubt and fear yesterday to see whether Germany and Russia will fly at each other's throats, all parties in Britain solemnly united to face the common peril of war. Mr Asquith and Mr Bonar Law told the House of Commons yesterday that parties had agreed for the moment to sink their differences.

Meanwhile strict measures of precaution, both naval and military, are being taken. Everything pointed to war on the Continent yesterday.

A German War Council sat through the night, Germans left Paris in hundreds for the Fatherland, and Berlin was wildly excited by reports, denied and then repeated, that mobilisation had been ordered.

In France the Premier was summoned to the President at 3.00am to prepare for eventualities. Germany, it was stated during the afternoon, demanded of Russia within 24 hours all explanation of her movements of troops. Failing a satisfactory answer, Germany, it is said, will respond by a counter mobilisation.

In Paris in the evening, however, it was believed that the situation had taken a turn for the better and that Germany was trying to bring Austria and Russia to an understanding.

"There is now a ray of hope," said M Viviani, the French Minister, when the news was received.

"We have just received from Germany news we did not even hope for," declared M Malvy, French Minister of the Interior.

BRITAIN'S GREAT OBJECT

In a crowded and silent House of Commons yesterday Sir Edward Grey spoke briefly and with deep gravity of the European situation.

"The outstanding facts," he said, "are much the same as yesterday. Austria has begun war against Servia, and Russia has ordered a partial mobilisation, which has not hitherto led to any corresponding steps by other Powers so far as our information goes.

"We continue to pursue one object – the preservation of European peace – and for this purpose we are keeping in close touch with the other Powers.

"In thus keeping in touch, we have, I am glad to say, had no difficulty."

BELGRADE IN FLAMES

HEAVY LOSSES IN FIERCE ALL-DAY BATTLE NEAR SERVIAN CAPITAL

The Servian Legation states that an official dispatch from Nish announces that the bombardment of Belgrade by Austro-Hungarian forces was resumed at six o'clock yesterday morning. The principal streets of Belgrade were shelled.

Berlin, 30 July – A message received in Berlin states that Belgrade is in flames. The message adds that an Austrian airman flew over the Servian lines and after reconnoitring the position returned to Neusatz.

FIGHT IN SERVIAN TERRITORY

Milan, 30 July – It is reported here that a great battle is now raging between the Servians and the Austrians on Servian territory to the south of Belgrade.

The battle, which started in the morning, continued all day, and fighting was going on at nightfall. The casualties are said to be heavy, but no advantage has been gained on either side.

AUSTRIANS REPULSED ON DANUBE

St Petersburg, 30 July – A telegram from Nish reports that an artillery battle has begun near Kieznicy and at Smederevo, some 20 miles south of Belgrade.

The Servian Legation has stated that in this battle, which was on a large scale, the Servians replied to the Austrian bombardment, and checked an attempt at crossing.

AUSTRIAN COLUMNS FIGHTING

Rome, 30 July – Dispatches from Nish, via Salonica, received here, state that yesterday the Austrians continued their advance on three different sides, and were met with sharp resistance from the small detachments of Servians which were left to obstruct their progress.

The Austrian column which began its advance up the Morava Valley encountered the Servs at Semendria. The Servs kept up a determined resistance until the nightfall, both sides sustaining heavy losses. Several hundreds were killed.

800 SERVIANS KILLED IN BATTLE

Berlin, 30 July – The *Tageszeitung* announces that a severe Servian defeat has taken place at Foca, adding that two Servian divisions were driven back by the Austrians, and that one division was surrounded and captured.

Eight hundred Servians are said to have been killed, while Austrian losses were reported as 200.

WHAT WILL GERMANY DO?

EXPLANATION OF RUSSIAN MOBILISATION DEMANDED WITHIN 24 HOURS

Berlin, 30 July – The *Deutsche Tageszeitung* learns on reliable authority that Germany has addressed to Russia a demand for an explanation of the Russian mobilisation and asked for a reply within 24 hours. The German Government has decided to secure a decisive answer, as she states that she will be unable to allow the continuance of these preparations without interfering.

GERMANY "NOT MOBILISING"

Paris, 30 July – *La Liberte* announces that the German Ambassador

7

Liberal Prime Minister Herbert Asquith in the days leading up to the declaration of war with Germany and the Austro-Hungarian Empire, July 1914.

in Paris visited the Quai d'Orsay this evening in order to declare officially that Germany had not mobilised and that direct negotiations were still going on between Vienna and St Petersburg.

KAISER'S ALL-NIGHT COUNCIL

Berlin, 30 July – At 9.00am today Berlin was without news of the decisions taken at the all-night Council of war at Potsdam, where the Kaiser sat in earnest conference with his political military and naval chieftains.

"DOING HER BEST FOR PEACE"

Reuter's Agency has received the following from a well-informed source:

"Despite any idea to the contrary, Germany is doing her best to prevent a European outbreak.

"She cannot bring pressure to bear upon her ally to stop all action, but she had been giving, and continues to give, good advice in Vienna.

"The partial mobilisation of Russia has made the situation as regards Germany, and particularly Austria, more difficult. Notwithstanding this, there is, in the German view, hope that a peaceful settlement can be reached."

GERMANY "WAITING FOR WAR"

Berlin, 30 July – "Waiting for war" sums up the condition of things in Germany today. Trains for France are beginning to bring in hundreds of Germans, including many women and children from Paris.

"FALSE NEWS"

Berlin, 30 July – It was a special edition of the *Lokal-Anzeiger* which erroneously announced the mobilisation of the army. Subsequently the journal published another special edition, in which it was stated:

"Owing to gross carelessness, special editions were published today stating that mobilisation had been ordered. We now state that this news is false."

WOMEN WHO SOBBED THEIR FAREWELLS

MOVING SCENES IN AUSTRIAN "WAR TRAIN" AND IN VIENNA

Vienna, 28 July, midnight (delayed in transmission) – War is a great leveller. Today I have seen how a mere declaration of war has been enough to bring to the same heights of pathetic resignation the high-born wife of an Austrian officer and the humblest peasant woman.

It began late last night, when my train was still in German territory. Two hours after leaving Frankfurt I noticed that third-class carriages had been added to our express, which had become a "war train". We were carrying Austrian reservists. At every stopping place little groups of reservists joined the train.

In every case they were accompanied by women-folk – stolid-looking peasant women, plainly dressed and worn down by much work and worry.

Little was said. The man, as a rule, contented himself with patting his wife's or sweetheart's arm, averting his eyes when he noticed that hers were over-running with tears as if her heart would break.

Because a war is only carried out by tears and broken hearts and, from what I saw two years ago in Servia and today in Germany, the men not only work but fain would weep.

These farewell partings of peasant men and women who had too much feeling and too little imagination to say much appealed even to station masters, who gave lovers that extra precious minute when if nothing more is said is yet sufficient for one last handshake and one last look.

In Vienna today there were pathetic scenes and to spare. It was the officer's last day out. The last promenade with his wife before going to war.

To understand the true significance of the fact it must be remembered that the one thing that delights the true Viennese more than anything in this world is to take his wife or sweetheart for a walk along the beautiful Ring – the world-famous boulevard of palaces.

Today the Viennese officer made his last appearance in the Ring. For the last time he walked along with his wife and she, despite an occasional twitching of lips and deep circles under the eyes which spoke of many tears, made as brave a show as she could.

Slowly they walked along – perhaps a little slower than usual – the sword clanking a little less than customary – the arm token held a little more firmly.

OFF TO WAR

In the same spirit the aged Archduke Frederick – with his pathetic likeness to the Emperor Francis Joseph – walked round the Ring this evening. He was accompanied by his young son, the Archduke Albrecht, the latter in deep mourning for the murdered heir and his consort.

The two Archdukes were surrounded by a large but very respectful crowd as they slowly proceeded along the "ceremony walk". Every hat was raised; every woman who passed made her curtsey as if accustomed to Court procedure.

And then there has been the departure of the troops. Thousands of men have marched through the city to the southern station to be drafted off to the war.

Despite the fact that the war is a cruel blow to trade and brought business to a standstill, despite the fact that there is a strict censorship even on private letters, nobody grumbles.

WAR MENACE SPOILS HOLIDAY ABROAD

ANXIOUS VISITORS LEAVE CONTINENT FOR ENGLAND – OTHERS, SEEKING ADVENTURE, SET OUT FOR AUSTRIA

These are rather anxious times for the tourist agencies and the railway companies booking passengers to the Continent and the Far East.

Large numbers of people who have been spending the summer on the Continent have become so nervous at the menace of war on all sides that they are hurriedly packing up their baggage and leaving for England. Elderly ladies who have sons or relatives holiday-making in Germany or Switzerland are writing urgent letters for them to come back to the safety of these shores.

"Please come home at once," runs a typical letter. "You are sure to get imprisoned or possibly tortured by those dreadful foreigners. I shall not have a minute's peace until I see you safely home again."

In response to demands such as these and also with a regard for their own safety, a great number of people are cutting short their Continental holiday and returning home as fast as they can to spend the rest of their vacation at some quiet English seaside resort.

1 August **1914**

WHAT THE NATIONS OF EUROPE ARE DOING

Austria – Army and Navy on war footing (Army: 2,500,000 men; Navy: 11 battleships, 7 cruisers, 19 destroyers, 58 torpedo boats, 10 submarines, 6 monitors on Danube).

Germany – believed to be mobilising, but no news allowed to leak out (Army: 5,000,000; Navy: 37 battleships, 13 battle cruisers, 48 cruisers, 142 destroyers, 47 torpedo boats, 27 submarines).

Russia – general mobilisation of Army and Navy (Army: 4,500,000; Navy: 8 battleships, 14 cruisers, 95 destroyers, 26 submarines).

Italy – no news forthcoming (Army: 750,000; Navy: 11 battleships, 16 cruisers, 36 destroyers, 70 torpedo boats, 18 submarines).

France – taking precautions, but not mobilising (Army: 4,000,000; Navy: 21 battleships [8 Dreadnoughts], 30 cruisers, 83 destroyers, 165 torpedo boats, 70 submarines).

Great Britain – every precaution, naval and military, being taken (Army, including troops in Possessions and Colonies: 800,000; Navy: 55 battleships, 7 battle cruisers, 120 cruisers, 191 destroyers, 109 torpedo boats, 70 submarines).

Holland – mobilised (Army about 500,000).

Switzerland – mobilised (Army about 250,000).

SMALL STATES MOBILISE

The Hague, 31 July – The Queen at half-past one today signed a decree ordering an urgent general mobilisation.

Berne, July 31 – The Federal Council ordered the mobilisation of the Landwehr and the Landsturm.

TO STAND AS ONE MAN

"If the occasion arises the New Zealand Government will ask the Parliament and people of New Zealand to do their duty by offering the services of an expeditionary force to the Imperial Government."

This important statement in the New Zealand House of Representatives was made by the Hon W F Massey, the Prime Minister, according to a telegram received yesterday by the High Commissioner in London.

"We have no fear of volunteers not being forthcoming," the Premier went on. "I may say an understanding has been arrived at with regard to the numbers and constitution of forces which will fit in with Imperial requirements, and I would like to add as far as domestic troubles are concerned I trust that a settlement will be arrived at which will enable the citizens of the Empire to stand together as one man.

"Just one word more with regard to Canada's offer, reported in tonight's papers. My opinion is that it may be summed up in these words, 'Well done, Canada!'"

CANADA'S CONTINGENT

Ottawa, 31 July – Mr Hughes, the Minister for War, says Canada can have 20,000 men on the transport ships within a fortnight of Great Britain announcing her participation in a European conflict.

The Tsar and the general staff of the Russian Army seen here in prayer following mobilisation of the Army, August 1914.

THE DAILY MIRROR, Saturday, August 1, 1914.

ORDER MONDAY'S GREAT HOLIDAY NUMBER OF THE DAILY MIRROR TO-DAY

The Daily Mirror

LATEST CERTIFIED CIRCULATION MORE THAN 1,000,000 COPIES PER DAY

No. 3,361. Registered at the G.P.O. as a Newspaper. SATURDAY, AUGUST 1, 1914 One Halfpenny.

"RUSSIA HAS MOBILISED AND GERMANY WILL FOLLOW SUIT" SAYS THE PREMIER: THE TSAR AS GENERALISSIMO AND THE COSSACKS HE WILL COMMAND.

The Tsar, on whom so much depends.

His Majesty wearing national dress.

The Cossacks are a most valuable element in the army—

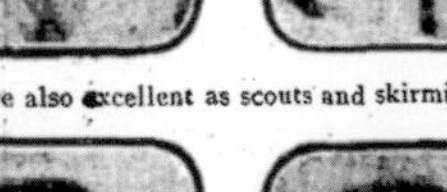

They are also excellent as scouts and skirmishers.

—And form a first-rate irregular cavalry.

A typical Cossack.

Their name signifies freebooter, adventurer or guerilla.

"We have just heard . . . that Russia has proclaimed a general mobilisation of her army and fleet . . . We understand this to mean that mobilisation will follow in Germany, if the Russian mobilisation is general and is proceeded with." This announcement was made in the House of Commons by Mr. Asquith yesterday, and so black is the situation that only a miracle, it would seem, can avert the great tragedy. In the event of war, the Tsar, it is reported, will act as generalissimo of his forces.

ULSTER MEN READY FOR SERVICE

Sir Edward Carson, in reply to a correspondent, has stated that if required by the Government a large body of Ulster volunteers will be willing and ready to give their services for home defence, and many will be willing to serve anywhere they are required.

REPORTED RUSSIAN MOBILISATION ORDER FOR ARMY AND NAVY

GERMANY UNDER MARTIAL LAW

"We have just heard, not from St Petersburg, but from Germany, that Russia has proclaimed a general mobilisation of her army and fleet. In consequence of this martial law has been proclaimed in Germany. We understand this to mean that mobilisation will follow in Germany, if the Russian mobilisation is general and is proceeded with."

In these words Mr Asquith, in the House of Commons yesterday afternoon, announced the most fateful news for the peace of Europe yet received. Germany has been proclaimed in a state of war by an Imperial decree. The exportation of anything that may serve a nation at war has been strictly prohibited.

Messages from Berlin ceased to arrive last night, and telephone communication between Germany and France, Denmark and Belgium was cut off. The international train was stopped on the Belgian frontier and not allowed to proceed.

LAST EFFORTS FOR PEACE

Paris, 31 July – It is stated that Great Britain, in agreement with France, continues to make the greatest efforts with a view to finding a basis of understanding between Russia and Austria.

Reuters Agency was informed last night that the French troops have been withdrawn slightly from the frontier to avoid the danger of a collision with German troops in the vicinity.

There is still no confirmation of the general Russian mobilisation which, it now appears, was announced by the German Ambassador in St Petersburg.

It is stated that the action of the Russian Government, which is the outcome of news of movements of foreign ships and troops near the Russian coasts and frontiers, does not amount to a general mobilisation.

NEGOTIATIONS REOPENED

Vienna, 31 July (6.30pm) – Conversations continue between the Russian and Austro-Hungarian diplomatists. The Russian Ambassador yesterday and today had prolonged interviews at the Ballplatz.

Though no detail of the conversations has transpired in the Press, it seems to be admitted again this evening that a European conflict is not inevitable.

COUNTRY UNDER MARTIAL LAW

Berlin, 31 July – In conformity with Paragraph 88 of the Constitution of the German Empire, Bavaria being excluded, the German Emperor has decreed a state of war. For Bavaria a similar decree will be issued.

In other words, martial law is proclaimed throughout Germany, except for the moment in Bavaria, which as an independent kingdom issues its own decree.

The "state of war" relates to all military measures on the frontier and for the protection of railways, the restriction of the working of the postal, telegraphic and railway services for the benefit of the military administration. Other consequences are the prohibition of the publication of the movements of troops and war material.

The Federal Council today agreed to the issue of three Imperial orders prohibiting the export of provisions, fodder and litter material, livestock, animal products, mechanically-propelled vehicles such as motor cars, motor bicycles and their parts, crude mineral oil, coal tar and oils derived from coal. The orders come into force at once.

FRONTIER TROOPS ASSEMBLING

Paris, 31 July – Germany continues to assemble her frontier troops and to fortify her strong places. Reconnaissance services have been established and very active patrols are guarding the frontier.

BATTLE OF SEMLIN

AEROPLANES AND SEARCHLIGHTS PLAY A BIG PART IN THE DANUBE FIGHT

Vienna, 31 July – A telegram from Semlin, dated the 28th, says:

"At ten minutes to eight this evening a fierce rifle fire began at the Sava Bridge.

"An Austrian aeroplane flew over the Servian position and lit it up with a searchlight.

"At the same time the howitzers shelled the entrenchments with such remarkable accuracy that the enemy were silenced.

"Towards 11 o'clock the monitors began playing their searchlights, which showed up the bridge and the enemy's troops

The Crown Prince of Germany seen reviewing his troops, 1914.

advancing. Our troops at once began a heavy fire.

"Under the glare of the searchlights the enemy offered a splendid mark.

"For a short time the enemy attempted to reply to our fire, but the machine guns made dreadful havoc in the ranks of the enemy, who eventually fled in disorder leaving numerous dead and wounded behind.

"The attempt to totally blow up the bridge failed."

DEFENDING THE CAPITAL TO THE LAST

Belgrade, 31 July – The Austrian bombardment of Belgrade began at nine this morning and lasted until noon. It was particularly directed at the east and centre of the town and did some damage to the cathedral.

The Austrians tried to cross the Sava by the railway bridge. The Servians replied by firing at them. The determination of the Servian forces seems to be to defend the town to the last extremity.

AUSTRIANS CHECKED

Nish (via Salonica), 31 July – Dispatches arriving from Semendria (near Belgrade) declare that up till last night the Austrians had not succeeded in forcing the pass which would give them access to the Morava Valley and thus open the direct road to Nish.

Two Austrian divisions, after an all-day engagement along the banks for the Drina, also failed to force the defile of Kovatch, which leads to Plevlje and Priepolje.

FRANCE

SAFEGUARDING THE FRONTIER

Paris, 31 July – A Council was held at the Elysée today to discuss the situation and to take all the necessary measures to assure the safety of the French frontier.

LINER AS CRUISER

Pairs, 31 July – The French liner *La Provence*, which was to have sailed from New York tomorrow, has been requisitioned by the French Government as an auxiliary cruiser and will be armed and manned at once.

ATTEMPT OF FRENCH TUNNEL

Lagny (Seine-et-Maine), 31 July – An attempt was made this afternoon to blow up the tunnel of Chalifert.

MOTOR CARS UNDER ESCORT

Paris, 31 July – At Bonn the frontier between Germany and France is guarded by troops. Bridges spanning the river are lined with soldiers, and automobiles passing from one side to the other are accompanied by a military escort of both nations.

FIRST EFFECTS OF WAR

WIRELESS RECALL TO GERMAN LINER

German shipping is already feeling seriously the effects of the crisis. The Hamburg-America liner *President Grant* was recalled to New York by wireless yesterday. She had left for Europe the day before. Three other great German liners have for the present postponed their sailings.

The Hamburg-America boats *Vaterland*, *Imperator* and *Amerika* have been ordered not to sail. The *Imperator* is to remain at Hamburg, the *Vaterland* is to stay at New York and the *Amerika* at Boston.

North German Lloyd liners now at New York have been ordered by cable from Berlin to remain in port, and the German steamer *Hohenfelde* has been told to remain where it is at Savannah. The German liner *Kybfels*, which arrived in the Tees yesterday, was ordered to return immediately to Bremen without loading.

At this season of the year the business of the leading American lines in London is usually heavy. Yesterday, however, it promised to beat all records, the offices of the great companies in Cockspur Street being besieged all through the day by Americans anxious to return home by the earliest boat.

3 August **1914**

GERMANY DECLARES WAR ON RUSSIA AND INVADES FRANCE

The Great European War has broken out. Germany has formally declared war on Russia and yesterday invaded France at two points.

Twenty thousand of her troops are reported to have suffered a severe repulse, and to have been driven back over the frontier with heavy losses.

One great coup has been effected by the German troops. The Grand Duchy of Luxemburg, whose neutrality had been granted by

THE DAILY MIRROR, Monday, August 3, 1914.

Germany Declares War on Russia and Invades France.

The Daily Mirror

LATEST CERTIFIED CIRCULATION MORE THAN 1,000,000 COPIES PER DAY

No. 3,362 — MONDAY, AUGUST 3, 1914 — 24 PAGES. — One Halfpenny

"THE SWORD IS FORCED INTO OUR HAND," SAYS THE KAISER, AND MAKES WAR ON RUSSIA AND FRANCE.

Deutschland und Oesterreich

Sie sollen uns nur kommen!

It is Armageddon. Germany has declared war on Russia and, it was reported yesterday, is massing troops on the French frontier. Britain is taking its holiday under a sense of appalling calamity and of impending destruction which makes one shudder to contemplate. On Saturday the Kaiser made a warlike speech, and said, "The sword is being thrust into our hand." Then the die was cast, and London learnt the dread news at supper time. The War Lord is seen wearing the uniform of the "Death's Head Hussars." The postcard, which has an enormous sale, shows a German and an Austrian soldier standing side by side. The inscription means "Let them all come."

Members of the French Foreign Legion at Ostend in Belgium following the outbreak of war, 1914.

Germany, together with other Powers, has been invaded.

The possession of Luxemburg destroys almost entirely the value of the long and formidable line of French fortresses from Verdun to Toul.

On the Russo-German frontier fighting has taken place at several points, and an actual Russian invasion of Germany is reported.

Italy has decided to remain neutral.

Two Cabinet meetings of momentous significance were held yesterday.

"GOOD GERMAN SWORD"

BERLIN WAR FEVER

Berlin, 1 August – The Kaiser, who addressed a huge crowd yesterday, again made a short speech from a window of the Palace today to the masses of people gathered all around below.

His Majesty, who was saluted with a frenzy of cheers, said he thanked the people for the love and loyalty they had displayed for him. If it came to war, his Majesty said, all party strife would cease, as they would all be German brothers and nothing more.

In time of peace one party or another may have attacked him, but he forgave them now from the bottom of his heart. The Emperor concluded by saying that he hoped that the good German sword would emerge victoriously from the war.

The Imperial Chancellor, speaking from a window of his residence to the crowds, said:

"We all stand round our Emperor, whatever our views or our faith may be. We can but win. Let us firmly trust in God, Who up to now has always granted us victory."

"TO THE LAST DROP OF BLOOD"

Patriotic demonstrations in the Lustgarten, outside the Imperial Palace, continued all yesterday afternoon. At half-past six, the German Emperor and Empress and Prince Adalbert appeared at the balcony of the Knights Hall. Amid bursts of thunderous cheers, his Majesty spoke the following words:

"A dark day has today broken over Germany. Envious persons are everywhere compelling us to just defence. The sword is being forced into our hand. I hope that, if in the last hour my efforts to bring our adversaries to see things in their proper light and to maintain peace do not succeed, we shall, with God's help, wield the sword in such a way that we can again sheath it with honour.

"A war would require enormous sacrifices of blood and property from the German people, but we would show our adversaries what it means to attack Germany. And I now commend you to God. Go to church. Kneel down before God and ask Him for help for our brave army."

PROCESSION SINGING SONGS

At a quarter to 12 today a great procession marched from Unter den Linden down the Wilhelmstrasse singing patriotic songs. The Chancellor appeared at the central window of the Congress Chamber and was received with vociferous cheers. When silence had been obtained Herr von Bethmann-Hollweg, speaking in firm, ringing tones, made the following speech:

"At this serious hour, in order to give expression to the feelings of your Fatherland, you have come to the house of Bismarck, who, with the Emperor William the First and Field-Marshal von Moltke, welded the German Empire together.

"We wished to go on living in peace in the empire that we have developed in 44 years of peaceful labour. The whole work of the Emperor has been devoted to the maintenance of peace.

"To the last hour he has worked for the peace of Europe – he is still working for it. Should all his efforts prove in vain, should the sword be forced into our hands, we shall take the field with a clear conscience and the knowledge that we did not seek war.

"We shall then wage war for our existence and for our national honour to the last drop of our blood.

"In the gravity of this hour I remind you of the words of Prince Friedrich Karl to the men of Brandenburg, 'Let your hearts beat to God, your fists on the enemy'."

CRISIS MEETINGS OF THE CABINET

Two momentous meetings of the Cabinet took place yesterday. The first began at 11 o'clock and did not end until 2.00pm. Every member was present and Ministers looked exceedingly grave as they left.

At 6.30 they met again to continue the discussion of the vital and critical problems which had occupied them during the morning. The matters under discussion fall under two general heads.

The Government are still engaged on a final attempt to avert or restrict a European war even now, at the 11th hour, but are also working at the completion of their own preparations in the event of a general conflagration.

NAVY READY

In these preparations, of course, the Navy plays an overwhelming part. Fortunately the crisis has arisen at a moment when the Navy is more usually efficient and ready to strike, and it may be said to be prepared for instant action, thanks to measures taken, of the extent of which the general public is largely unaware.

There is reason to believe that the completion of these preparations was the principal topic under discussion at the morning meeting of the Cabinet. A Sunday meeting of the Cabinet is an event unprecedented in modern British history.

Large crowds gathered to watch the Ministers arrive, and police had to be summoned to clear Downing Street and prevent passage of all but those whose business required that they should go through.

A constant stream of dispatches from Government offices arrived at Downing Street while the Cabinet was in session. Before the Cabinet meeting Mr Asquith was visited by Mr Harcourt, Mr McKinnon Wood, Mr Pease, Mr Runciman and the Attorney-General, together with the German Ambassador – a most unusual visitor to No 10 – who on leaving crossed to the Foreign Office. Mr Alfred de Rothschild, the financier, also called.

Soon after the assemblage of Ministers, Sir William Tyrell, Sir Edward Grey's principal private secretary, hurried across from the Foreign Office with a typewritten document.

LATEST WAR NEWS FROM THE FRONTIERS

Germany, without declaration of war, invaded France at two points on the frontier – at Cirey (near Luneville, between the French fortresses of Nancy and Belfort) and Longwy (near the town of Luxemburg).

Twenty thousand Germans are reported (from Liege, near the Belgian frontier) to have been repulsed with heavy loss, after having crossed the French frontier near Nancy.

Germans have invaded Luxemburg, a neutral State, and, by advancing through it, can get behind the formidable line of French fortresses from Verdun to Toul. Luxemburg lies at the junction of the French, German and Belgian frontiers.

Russians have invaded Germany at Schwidden.

French airman stated to have dropped bombs near city of Nuremberg.

INVASION AT TWO POINTS

Reuters Agency is informed that at 3.30 yesterday afternoon an official telegram was received announcing the fact that the Germans had invaded France and crossed the frontier at Cirey-les-Forges (near Luneville, between the French fortresses of Nancy and Belfort).

Reuter's Agency is informed that another official telegram has been received announcing that a German force is marching on the French fortress of Longwy (18 mines WSW of Luxemburg).

LUXEMBURG INVADED

NEUTRALITY OF GRAND DUCHY VIOLATED BY GERMAN TROOPS

Luxemburg, 2 August – The German troops have entered the Grand Duchy of Luxemburg and have seized the Government offices. Telephone communication has been cut.

A train full of German soldiers arrived at the station of Luxemburg during the night. The troops seized the station and the bridges on the Treves and Trois Viarges lines in order to ensure the regular passage of military trains across the Grand Duchy.

Soldiers then proceeded to the barracks. The major commanding the detachment of Luxemburg volunteers there parleyed with them, protesting against this violation of neutrality. The Germans eventually withdrew, and a body of their officers proceeded to the Palace of the Government. They had the court officials summoned, and they are now conferring with them.

The Germans assert that the railway lines belong to them, and that they have the right to do what they like. They refuse to withdraw.

Luxemburg is only a tiny State with 1,000 square miles of territory and 250,000 inhabitants. Its army consists of 200 men and six horses.

But its strategic importance is tremendous, behind the formidable fortified zone which protects the French frontier from Verdun to Toul.

The French works at Montmedy and Mexieres, which have recently been planned to meet such an attack, are believed to be not yet complete.

The invasion of Luxemburg is a direct violation of the Treaty of London (1867), which guaranteed forever the neutrality of the Grand Duchy. Article 2 of the treaty runs as follows:

"The Grand Duchy of Luxemburg will be a State perpetually neutral. The Powers which have signed the present treaty declare to be bound to respect this neutrality and to make it respected by others. This neutrality is placed under the sanction and the guarantee of the Powers which have signed this treaty."

Among the Powers which signed the treaty was Germany, and her coup is a grave breach of international law.

France has undertaken to respect Belgian neutrality, but the German Foreign Secretary declined, it is stated, to make any such promise when asked to do so by the British Ambassador in Berlin.

NOT A HOSTILE ACT

It is officially announced that the Luxemburg Minister of State

Every man who returns to the capital from Liege is regarded as a hero and is made to tell again and again the wonderful story of how the Germans were repulsed by a heroic little band of defenders, August 1914.

THE MOTOR IN WAR: DEADLY WEAPONS WHICH MAY BE USED BY THE COMBATANTS.

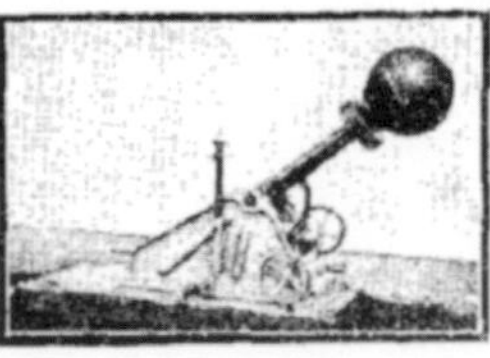

Armoured motor-car. An armoured gun and motor-car. The bomb-gun.

Will these modern weapons, in which the motor-car plays so important a part, be used in the great struggle? The armoured motor-car is Russia's, the motor gun-carriage and bomb-gun being Germany's. The last-named is most destructive, and fills the air with poisoned gases.

has received a telegram from the German Imperial Chancellor stating that the military measures taken by the Germans in Luxemburg do not constitute a hostile act against the Grand Duchy.

They are simply measures taken to protect the working of the railways connected with the German system against a possible attack by French troops.

Luxemburg will be completely indemnified for any damage that may be done to the lines.

ITALY TO BE NEUTRAL

BOUND TO GERMANY AND AUSTRIA ONLY BY DEFENSIVE ALLIANCE

Paris, 1 August – It is authoritatively announced that the Marquis di San Giuliano, the Italian Minister for Foreign Affairs, has informed the German Ambassador in Rome that Italy will remain neutral.

Her obligations under the Triple Alliance only applying to a defensive war, Italy considers herself to be released from her engagements, the war waged by Austria, supported by Germany, being an essentially offensive war.

Italy's decision to remain neutral is of more importance than it might seem at first sight. She has only nine battleships, of which eight are pre-Dreadnoughts. This fleet would not be a very valuable addition to the navies of the Germanic Powers.

But the damage she might inflict with her torpedo boats and the necessity of threatening her coasts in order to weaken her forces at the seat of the land war would mean a serious increase in the naval responsibilities of France and Great Britain.

JAPAN TO BE NEUTRAL?

Tokyo, 2 August – The Japanese Premier is reticent regarding Japan's attitude, because war between Austria-Hungary and Servia does not affect peace in the Far East.

If, however, England should participate in a European war Japan may have to declare a benevolent neutrality.

DEMOLISHING BELGRADE

UNINTERRUPTED BOMBARDMENT OF CITY, WHICH HAS BEEN LEFT DEFENCELESS

Nish (provisional Servian capital), 30 July – It is learned from Servian official sources that the bombardment of Belgrade is proceeding uninterruptedly. The Austrians are using siege guns with the intention of demolishing the city. Belgrade is divided into sections.

Many have been killed by the bombardment, which began with the greatest suddenness, and the damage is incalculable.

The inhabitants have not left the city, which has never been summoned to surrender.

It is reported that the ironworks, the tobacco factory and even the cathedral have been destroyed by the bombardment.

ALL SOLDIERS WITHDRAWING

According to a telegram received at the Servian Embassy in London on Sunday, the bombardment of Belgrade took place at a time when the town was absolutely defenceless, every soldier having left three days before.

The Austrian shells did much damage to a number of private and public buildings, among them the British Legation.

The beautiful public park of Belgrade (the Hyde Park of the Servian capital) suffered considerably, as did the main street.

The first Servian shot was not fired from Belgrade, as reported, but from a point much higher up the river, where Servian soldiers were attempting to prevent the Austrians from effecting a crossing.

Instead of replying at that point, the Austrians commenced the bombardment.

➧ Russian citizens holding banners declaring freedom for the country and support for the Tsar and the Army following the declaration of war against Germany and the Hapsburg Empire, August 1914.

WOMEN IN CHEERING PROCESSIONS

St Petersburg, 1 August – The declaration of war by Germany was communicated to the public about half-past nine this evening and provoked everywhere great demonstration of patriotic enthusiasm.

The capital this evening presents a spectacle of extraordinary animation. The streets are filled with people, especially in the principal streets, where groups collect and eagerly read the special editions of the newspapers.

On the Nevsky Prospekt, where the crowd is particularly dense,

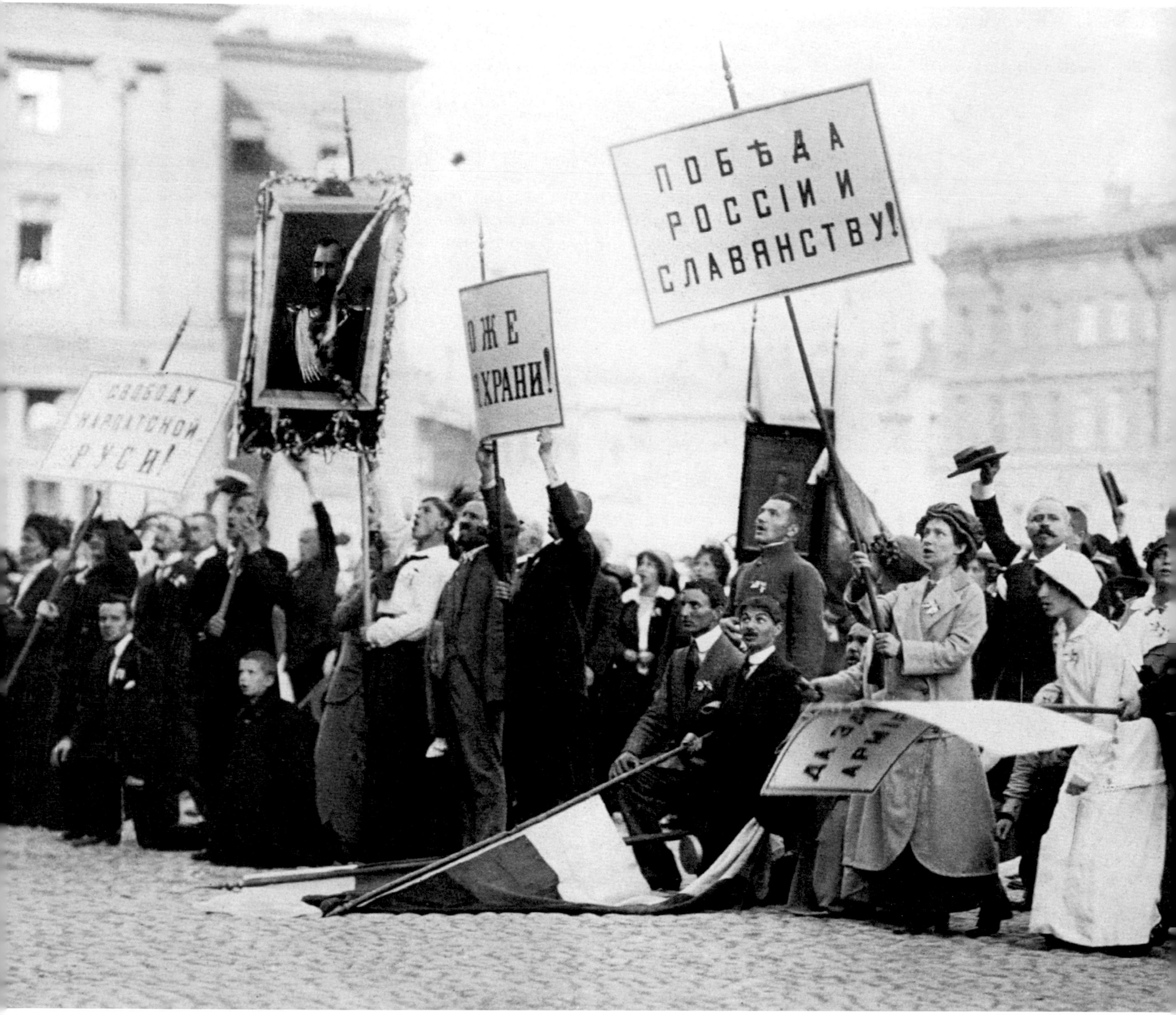

all classes of society are participating in the patriotic outburst.

Women carrying children are to be seen in the processions, bearing flags and portraits of the Tsar, at the sight of which the throng burst into loud cheering. From time to time the processionists halt to allow a speaker to give an extempore harangue, full of patriotic fervour.

In front of the Kazan Cathedral a sudden hush falls upon the crowd, and then the strains of the national anthem sung in perfect harmony by a section of the procession rise on the air, the crowd listening with bared heads and in perfect silence.

On its conclusion the demonstrations are renewed with greater ardour than ever. The Servian Legation and the French and British Embassies were the objects of particularly warm demonstrations.

CROWD'S FRENZIED JOY

Berlin, 31 July (delayed in transmission) – During the afternoon a constant stream of people flocked to Unter den Linden and took up their stand there. Tens of thousands of all ranks and conditions of men, women and children gathered on the pavements and greeted with enthusiastic shouts the royal personages and other notabilities who passed along on their way to the castle.

A crowd of 50,000 gathered in front of the castle and raised continuous cheers for the Sovereign and the Empire. Between the rounds of cheers well-known patriotic songs were sung until, at a given moment, the Emperor appeared at a window and delivered a speech.

His Majesty's appearance was the signal for a perfect tornado of cheering. At the conclusion of his speech his Majesty bowed low his thanks to the people and then withdrew, followed by the shouts of the enthusiastic throng.

RUSH TO THE FRONTIER FROM PARIS, WHICH REMAINS CALM

POSITION OF ENGLISH IN THE CITY

Paris, 2 August – War! It has come at last. At least, it appears to have come, for the difference between a general mobilisation and a state of war is hardly apparent. Soldiers are leaving for the frontier by every train, sobbing women and children are bidding them goodbye with many a fond embrace and wondering whether they will ever see them again.

Nothing like this has been seen in Paris for 40 years, and the recurrence of the conditions which prevailed before the war of 1870 fires every military man in France with the hope that this is the long-wished-for opportunity for "La Revanche". As soon as the mobilisation order was posted up on the walls of Paris there was an immediate cessation of street traffic.

WHEELED TRAFFIC STOPS

An immense number of motor cabs and all motor-omnibuses in Paris were commandeered, and tonight it is almost impossible to hire a cab anywhere in the city. Wheeled traffic was never so scarce on the boulevards as it is tonight, for all the horses are in the hands of the military, and the omnibuses are being used for transport purposes.

The attitude of Parisians since the issue of the mobilisation order has been admirable. At six o'clock this evening a procession numbering several thousands marched along the boulevards, with French, Russian and English flags, singing the "Marseillaise".

There was no rowdyism; only a desire to demonstrate their enthusiasm at the prospect of coming to grips with the hated German.

I have been astonished at the calm of my French confreres who are ordered to the front. One of them, a big, black-bearded giant, who is now on his way to join an artillery regiment at Belfort, reasoned out the situation with all the calm of a practised philosopher.

"With shrapnel," he said, "you need not worry. Either you are dead before you know or it passes you by and leaves you scathless."

ENGLISH PEOPLE IN FRANCE

All foreigners may leave Paris or France before the end of the first day of mobilisation by train, but not automobile. Those desiring to leave France may do so by certain trains on a time-table posted on the walls of Paris, or by sea.

Americans and English may remain in France except in the regions of the eastern frontier and certain fortresses, provided they make a declaration to the police and obtain a special permit.

No foreigner is permitted to leave France after the first day of mobilisation without a passport signed by a prefect.

Americans, English and other foreigners may remain in Paris by obtaining a special permit.

Exception is made in the case of Austrians, who will be taken to special refuge depots in Western France, where they will be lodged.

Anyone breaking these rules will immediately be arrested.

➧ On the day of German mobilisation young, enthusiastic Germans take to the streets singing national songs, while soldiers parade through the streets of Berlin, 2 August 1914.

The Conflict Escalates into Global Hostilities

4 August **1914** – 7 August **1914**

With Germany having violated the neutrality of Belgium, Great Britain was left with no option other than to declare war on Germany. Within days, Servia and France had joined the British in their fight against the Germans and the world was at war.

The largest conflict of the 20th century so far may have utilised modern technology in the form of aircraft and motorised vehicles, but the military was still heavily biased towards traditional forms of warfare such as these mounted Belgian Lancers, 28 September 1914.

4 August **1914**

GREAT BRITAIN DECLARES WAR ON GERMANY

Declaration last night after "unsatisfactory reply" to British ultimatum that Belgium must be kept neutral.

THE KING'S MESSAGE TO HIS NAVY

Government to take control of all railways. Admiral Jellicoe to be in supreme command of the Home Fleets.

HUGE CROWDS CHEER THEIR MAJESTIES AT PALACE

£100,000,000 voted in Commons in five minutes. German invasion of Belgium with airships.

Great Britain is in a state of war with Germany. It was officially stated at the Foreign Office last night that Great Britain declared war against Germany at 7pm. The British Ambassador in Berlin has been handed his passport.

War was Germany's reply to our request that she should respect the neutrality of Belgium, whose territories we were bound in honour and by treaty obligations to maintain inviolate.

Speaking in a crowded and hushed House the Premier yesterday afternoon made the following statement: "We have made a request to the German Government that we shall have a satisfactory assurance as to the Belgian neutrality before midnight tonight."

The German reply to our request, officially stated last night, was unsatisfactory.

THE KING AND HIS NAVY

The King has addressed the following message to Admiral Sir John Jellicoe: "At this grave moment in our national history I send to you and, through you, to the officers and men of the fleets, of which you have assumed command, the assurance of my confidence that under your direction they will revive and renew the old glories of the Royal Navy, and prove once again the sure shield of Britain and of her Empire in the hour of trial."

The above message has been communicated to the senior naval officers on all stations outside of home waters.

It was reported yesterday evening that Germany had taken the first hostile step by destroying a British mine-layer.

At the present time Germany is in a state of war with: Great Britain, Russia, France and Belgium.

It would seem as if Germany, in her ambition to control the destiny of the whole of Europe, were ready to embark on any grandiose scheme of adventure, however precarious her chances.

So far as Great Britain is concerned, her attitude has always been plain, straightforward and perfectly intelligible. She was prepared to stand aside from the conflict that has now involved practically the whole of Europe.

But she insisted and had to insist on two things: these were that Belgium's neutrality should be respected; and that the German fleet should not bombard defenceless French towns.

Germany tried to bribe us with peace to desert our friends and duty. But Great Britain has preferred the path of honour.

CHIEF OF THE FLEETS

Sir John R Jellicoe has assumed the supreme command of the Home Fleets, with the acting rank of Admiral. Rear Admiral Charles E Madden has been appointed to be his chief of staff. Field Marshal Sir John French, the famous cavalry leader, has been appointed Inspector General to the Forces.

Mr Lloyd George subsequently announced in the House that the Government was engaged in preparing a scheme for the distribution of food, and hoped that it would be completed in the course of one or two days. The House unanimously passed in five minutes all outstanding votes, amounting to over £100,000,000.

An Order in Council has been issued declaring it expedient that Government should have control over the railroads of Great Britain.

ROARS OF CHEERS FOR THE KING

The King and Queen, accompanied by the Prince of Wales and Princess Mary, were hailed with wild, enthusiastic cheers when they appeared at about eight o'clock last night on the balcony of Buckingham Palace, before which a record crowd had assembled.

Seeing the orderliness of the crowd, the police did not attempt to force the people back and went away.

A little later the police passed the word around that silence was necessary as the King was holding a meeting in the Palace, and except for a few spasmodic outbursts there was silence for a time.

Afterwards the cheering was renewed with increased vigour and soon after 11pm the King and Queen and Prince of Wales made a further appearance on the balcony and the crown once more sang the National Anthem, following this with hearty clapping and cheering.

After the departure of the royal party some minutes later many of the crowd dispersed. Several enthusiasts, however, stayed outside keeping up the demonstration by shouting and waving flags.

THE DAILY MIRROR, Tuesday, August 4, 1914.

Success of Our New Serial, "The Influence of a Girl": See page 11.

The Daily Mirror

LATEST CERTIFIED CIRCULATION MORE THAN 1,000,000 COPIES PER DAY

No. 3,363. Registered at the G.P.O. as a Newspaper. TUESDAY, AUGUST 4, 1914 One Halfpenny.

KING GEORGE SIGNS THE ARMY MOBILISATION ORDER: THE FRENCH COAST PROTECTED BY THE BRITISH FLEET.

The thoughts of all Britishers went out to sea yesterday, for with the statement of Sir Edward Grey in Parliament, the safety and sanctity of the Empire may easily again depend upon the Navy which has given us so heroic a history. Britain's position was clearly outlined by the Foreign Secretary. France's fleet was concentrated in the Mediterranean, as an act of friendship to England. If her enemy's fleet sails down the English Channel to attack the coast of France, we cannot stand aside. Sir Edward also announced that the mobilisation of the Army is taking place, but we have not taken any engagement to send an expeditionary army abroad.

Tuesday 8 p.m. August 4th 1914

[Form to be used when the whole of the Army Reserve is called out.]

Army Form D. 427.

GENERAL MOBILIZATION

Army Reserve

(REGULAR AND SPECIAL RESERVISTS).

HIS MAJESTY THE KING has been graciously pleased to direct by Proclamation that the Army Reserve be called out on permanent service.

ALL REGULAR RESERVISTS are required to report themselves at once at their place of joining in accordance with the instructions on their identity certificates for the purpose of joining the Army.

ALL SPECIAL RESERVISTS are required to report themselves on such date and at such places as they may be directed to attend for the purpose of joining the Army. If they have not received any such directions, or if they have changed their address since last attendance at drill or training, they will report themselves at once, by letter, to the Adjutant of their Unit or Depot.

The necessary instructions as to their joining will then be given.

4514 100,000 11—11 Forms D. 427 / 11
8 14 55

Printed for H. M. Stationery Office by Hazell, Watson & Viney, Ld., 52, Long Acre, London, W.C.

The General Mobilisation order issued by the UK Government on 4 August 1914, shortly after Britain had declared war on Germany following their invasion of Belgium.

Crowds cheer Prime Minister Herbert Asquith as he returns from Parliament following the declaration of war on 4 August 1914.

WHY THERE IS WAR

The following statement was issued from the Foreign Office last night: Owing to the summary rejection by the German Government of the request made by His Majesty's Government for assurances that the neutrality of Belgium would be respected, His Majesty's Ambassador in Berlin has received his passport, and His Majesty's Government has declared to the German Government that a state of war exists between Great Britain and Germany as from 11pm on August 4.

CALL FOR ALL MOTORCYCLISTS

The War Office announce that civilian medical practitioners desiring to serve at home or abroad as surgeons with the army should communicate with the Secretary, War Office.

Motorcyclists for service with the army are also required. Their pay will be 35s weekly, all found. A bounty of £10 will be paid to each man approved and a further £5 on discharge.

Men are required to enlist for one year, or as long as the

A PROCLAMATION
A PROCLAMATION
BY THE KING
A PROCLAMATION

war continues. A certain number of foreman artificers, electricians, blacksmiths etc, are also required for service with the army.

PRINCE ALBERT AT SEA

It is understood that the King yesterday received a telegram from his son Prince Albert, who is in the battleship *Collingwood*.

BRITISH WARSHIP REPORTED SUNK BY GERMAN FLEET

The alleged destruction of a British mine-layer was reported by the Press Association last night. It is understood, says the agency, that the British Government has received intimation of the sinking of a British mine-layer by the German fleet.

BRITAIN COMMANDEERS WARSHIPS

The Admiralty last night officially stated that the Government had taken over the two battleships, one completed and the other shortly due for completion, which had been ordered in this country by the Turkish Government and the two destroyer leaders ordered by the Government of Chile.

The two battleships will receive the names *Agincourt* and *Erin*, and the destroyer leaders will be called *Faulkner* and *Broke*, after two famous naval officers.

◀ Men reading the mobilisation proclamation on the declaration of war, 4 August 1914.

BATTLE OF BELGIUM

Germany has declared war on Belgium and invaded the country.

The Germans have entered Belgium, says an Exchange special message, at three places – Dolhain, Francorchamps and Stavelot.

An engagement is reported before Fort Fleron, Liège, and Visé, says the Central News, has been captured by the Germans. (Liège, on the Meuse, is a provincial city and the centre of the Belgian coalfields.

It exports firearms to every country in the world. Stavelot is 12 miles south-south east of Verviers. Francorchamps is two or three miles north of Stavelot. Visé, a town of 4,000 inhabitants, lies on the River Meuse, some 14 miles inside the Belgian frontier. It is about equidistant from Verviers and Maastricht.)

The Belgian Legation in London had informed Mr Asquith that Belgian territory had been violated at Verviers, near Aix-la-Chapelle, and that a German force had penetrated still further into Belgian territory.

Berlin, August 4 – It is announced here that a portion of the garrison of Memel, on the east Prussian frontier, yesterday repulsed an advance party of the enemy's frontier guards. (Reuters)

Berlin, August 4 – A Bill was presented in the Reichstag today authorising the Imperial Chancellor to raise a credit of five milliards of marks – about 250 millions sterling – to meet non-recurring extraordinary expenditure.

AIRMEN'S BOMBS AS CAUSE OF WAR

The Daily Mirror's Paris correspondent states that before Baron von Schoen, the German Ambassador, left Paris he told Monsieur Viviani that Germany considered herself in a state of war with France, and the reason for it was because French airmen had dropped bombs on Nuremberg.

Paris, August 4 – Shortly before 6pm yesterday evening a German aeroplane dropped three bombs in the town of Luneville. Some damage was done, but there were no casualties.

Paris, August 3 – The French Government formally denies the report that French officers disguised as Ublans have penetrated into German territory.

QUIET GERMAN EMBASSY

Absolute quiet prevailed at the German Embassy at 11.15pm last night, though earlier in the evening there had been some booing.

The Ambassador sat in his room on the lower floor writing dispatches. The window was open and the room was fully lighted. At 11.30pm he finished and his butler came to close the window and put out the lights.

As the clock struck 12 the few people still outside the Embassy began to suggest that the Ambassador had departed. In response to an enquiry by *The Daily Mirror* the butler smilingly replied, "The people are mistaken – the Ambassador has gone to bed."

The German Ambassador leaves today.

August 4, 12.13am – Reuters Agency is informed that it is now stated officially at the Foreign Office that it was Great Britain who declared war against Germany at 7pm this evening.

THE DAILY MIRROR, Wednesday, August 5, 1914.

GREAT BRITAIN DECLARES WAR ON GERMANY.

The Daily Mirror

LATEST CERTIFIED CIRCULATION MORE THAN 1,000,000 COPIES PER DAY

No. 3,364. Registered at the G.P.O. as a Newspaper. WEDNESDAY, AUGUST 5, 1914 One Halfpenny.

DECLARATION OF WAR BY GREAT BRITAIN AFTER UNSATISFACTORY REPLY TO YESTERDAY'S ULTIMATUM.

Neptune's imps. They are torpedo-boats steaming in close order to enable them to send verbal messages one to another by means of a megaphone.

Field-Marshal Sir John French.

Rear-Admiral C. E. Madden.

Admiral Sir John Jellicoe.

Field-Marshal Earl Kitchener.

Remarkable picture of a submarine rising to the surface. Are we soon to know what these unknown quantities are capable of?

There are four men—two sailors and two soldiers—to whom the Empire will turn in her hour of need. The sailors are Admiral Sir John Jellicoe (known as "the future Nelson"), who has assumed supreme command of the Home Fleets with the acting rank of Admiral, and Rear-Admiral Charles E. Madden, who has been appointed to be his Chief of Staff. The soldiers are Lord Kitchener, whose achievements are known to everyone, and Sir John French, probably the finest cavalry leader in the world, who performed brilliant feats in South Africa, "the grave of reputations."—(Bassano, Symonds, Russell and Gale and Polden.)

5 August **1914**

BRITAIN IN A STATE OF WAR WITH GERMANY

WAR SITUATION AT A GLANCE

Great Britain has delivered to Germany an ultimatum expiring at midnight. We require a satisfactory declaration on the subject of Belgium's neutrality, which we are in honour bound to defend.

It is now definitely known that Germany has invaded and declared war against Belgium because the latter country would not violate its obligations of neutrality.

Apart from such action as we may be compelled by circumstances to adopt, the nations at present at war are:

* Austria against Servia
* Germany against France
* Germany against Russia
* Germany against Belgium

Practically every country in Europe is today mobilised, and not less than 12,000,000 men are under arms.

A sum of £100,000,000 was yesterday voted in five minutes in the House of Commons.

PRIME MINISTER'S MOMENTOUS DECLARATION IN COMMONS

Reuters learns that a state of war exists between Great Britain and Germany. This momentous announcement was received last night. It was the sequel to the Premier's statement in the House yesterday that "We have made a request to the German Government that we shall have a satisfactory assurance as to Belgian neutrality before midnight tonight (Tuesday)."

It was Britain's ultimatum to Germany and the news was received with deafening cheers by a thronged and excited Chamber.

MR ASQUITH'S GRAVE STATEMENT

In a strained silence in every part of the House of Commons yesterday, the Prime Minister made his momentous statement. He explained how the King of the Belgians had appealed to England for diplomatic intervention on behalf of his country, Germany having demanded free passage for her troops through Belgium, promising to maintain the integrity and independence of the kingdom.

"Simultaneously," concluded Mr Asquith, "we received from the Belgian Legation in London the following telegram from the Belgian Minister for Foreign Affairs:

'The General Staff announce that territory has been violated at Verviers, near Aix-la-Chapelle. Subsequent information tends to show that a German force has penetrated still further into Belgian territory.'

"We also received this morning from the German Ambassador here a telegram sent to him from the German Foreign Secretary:

'Please dispel any distrust that must exist on the part of the British Government with regard to our intentions by repeating, most positively, the formal assurance that, even in the case of armed conflict with Belgium, Germany will not, under any pretence whatever, annex Belgian territory.

'Please impress upon Sir Edward Grey that the German Army could not be exposed to a French attack across Belgium, which was planned according to absolutely unimpeachable information.'

"I have," continued Mr Asquith, "to add this on behalf of the Government: 'We cannot regard this as in any sense a satisfactory communication.'

"We have, in reply to it, repeated the request we made last week to the German Government that they should give us the same assurance with regard to Belgian neutrality as was given to us and to Belgium by France last week.

"We have asked that a reply to that request and a satisfactory answer to the telegram of this morning, which I have read to the House, should be given before midnight."

CALM AND UNITED EMPIRE

The King has sent the following message to his Colonies:

"I desire to express to my people of the Oversea Dominions with what appreciation and pride I have received the messages from their respective Governments during the last few days.

"These spontaneous assurances of their fullest support recall to me the generous, self-sacrificing help given by them in the past to the mother country.

"I shall be strengthened in the discharge of the great responsibility which rests upon me by the confident belief that in this time of trial my Empire will stand united, calm and resolute, trusting in God" *George RI.*

CORSAGES

French Dragoon cavalrymen leaving Paris on 5 August 1914 following the declaration of war.

BELGIUM MOBILISES: WILL "EUROPE'S COCKPIT" SEE ANOTHER WATERLOO?

SAILORS CALM AMID WOMEN'S TEARS

SOBBED FAREWELLS TO NAVAL RESERVISTS – ONLY CHILDREN HAPPY

Remarkable mobilisation scenes took place at all the railway stations yesterday. During the day a constant stream of trains left with the announcement "For Seamen Only" posted on the carriages. All the men belonged to the Royal Navy Reserves. Hardly any of them arrived at the stations unaccompanied by friends or relatives.

Many pathetic scenes of farewell took place. The sailors were calm and even cheerful but mothers, wives, sisters and sweethearts broke down repeatedly and sobbed. Young children were, perhaps, the happiest persons present. They knew nothing of the grave nature of the occasion, and apparently thought they were taking part in a holiday.

In the streets uniformed men were to be seen everywhere, all very brisk, eager and cheerful.

At places like Piccadilly Circus and Trafalgar Square, crowds raised cheers as members of the forces went by while strangers stopped them repeatedly, shook them by the hand and wished them luck. A Strand barber insisted upon three sailors who had come in for a shave accepting free shampoos as well. Meanwhile remarkable recruiting scenes were being witnessed.

PROMISING MATERIAL

Great crowds collected outside the Central Recruiting Office in Great Scotland Yard and watched a constant stream of would-be recruits enter the building. A sergeant on duty said large detachments of the men looked very promising material.

At the headquarters of the County of London Territorial Regiment in Chelsea another rush was experienced. One of the most striking instances of the day was the way in which the crowd outside Wellington Barracks saluted the guards' colours. When the guards marched on to the parade ground the great crowd of civilians present bared their heads before the flag that is so famous in our Army's heroic history.

In response to an appeal by the Marquis of Tullibardine for the names of aviators who would offer their services to the country a splendid list of volunteers was received by the Government yesterday.

"The pick of the flying talent of the country have placed themselves at the nation's service," said Lord Tullibardine.

URGENT CALL TO RESERVISTS

A general mobilisation having been proclaimed, all Regular Reservists, it was officially announced yesterday, are required to proceed immediately to the places of joining shown on their identity certificate without waiting for the receipt of their official notices to join.

On presenting the cash order on his identity certificate at the nearest post office (money order office) the Reservist will receive 3s

advance of pay. The railway or steamboat company will issue him a ticket to his place of joining when he presents the railway warrant on his identity certificate at the booking office.

It is of the utmost importance in the present emergency that every Regular reservist should join at the earliest possible moment, and His Majesty's Government rely with confidence upon railway and other transport companies, employers and the Reservists themselves to do all in their power to facilitate rapid mobilisation.

Officers on leave and warrant officers, non-commissioned officers and men on furlough are also required to return to their units or appointments at once without waiting for orders.

ECONOMY FOR THE SAKE OF THE POOR

An appeal to the prosperous in England to be economical in their use of meat during the present times of crisis was endorsed by Mr Asquith yesterday in the House of Commons.

He was asked by Mr Bathurst whether, in view of the comparative scarcity and high price of meat, the Government will consider the desirability of appealing to the more prosperous classes in England to economise, for the sake of their poorer fellow-citizens.

In reply the Prime Minister said: "I endorse the Honourable Member's appeal. It is, in my opinion, applicable to all classes of people and to all kinds of foodstuffs."

THE KING'S APPEAL

MESSAGE TO TSAR IN LAST EFFORT TO PREVENT WAR

The text of the King's message to the Tsar – the final effort on the British side to preserve the world's peace – was issued last night. On 1 August at 3.30am, Sir Edward Grey telegraphed to Sir G Buchanan, the British Ambassador in St Petersburg, instructing him to apply for an audience with the Tsar and to convey to him a personal message from King George.

In this message his Majesty detailed the Kaiser's efforts at mediation between Austria and Russia, his telegram to the Tsar treating Russia's mobilisation as a hostile act, Germany's ultimatum to Russia, and her request to France to know if she would remain neutral during a German-Russian war. The King continued thus:

"I cannot help thinking that some misunderstanding has produced this deadlock. I am most anxious not to miss any possibility of avoiding the terrible calamity which at present threatens the whole world.

"I therefore make a personal appeal to you to remove the misapprehension which I feel must have occurred, and to leave still open grounds for negotiation and possible peace.

"If you think I can in any way contribute to that all-important purpose, I will do everything in my power to assist in reopening the interrupted conversations between the Powers concerned.

"I feel confident that you are as anxious as I am that all that is possible should be done to secure the peace of the world."

The Tsar in his reply said: "I would gladly have accepted your proposals had not German Ambassador this afternoon presented a Note to my Government declaring war.

"Every proposal, including that of your Government, was rejected by Germany and Austria. Austria's declaration of war on Servia forced me to order a partial mobilisation, though, in view of threatening situation, my military advisers strongly advised a general mobilisation, owing to quickness with which Germany can mobilise in comparison with Russia.

"I was eventually compelled to take this course . . . That I was justified in doing so is proved by Germany's sudden declaration of war. In this solemn hour," concluded the Tsar, "I wish to assure you once more that I have done all in my power to avert war. Now that it has been forced upon me, I trust your country will not fail to support France and Russia. God bless and protect you."

6 August **1914**

WAR GAINS AND LOSSES AT A GLANCE

The positions at the time of going to press of the campaigns waged by the seven nations now at war was as follows:

- ⋆ England and Germany – Naval battle stated to be in progress in the North Sea. Many German merchant ships captured.
- ⋆ France and Germany – French warships have captured a German cruiser, and there are reports that the German cruisers *Goeben* and *Breslau* have been captured and the cruiser *Panther* (of Agadir fame) sunk.
- ⋆ Germany and Belgium – After heroic fighting Belgians have forced a German Army of 80,000 to retire.
- ⋆ Germany and Russia – Russian cavalry repulsed with heavy losses near Saldan.
- ⋆ Austria and Servia – Austria reported to have crossed the Danube.

LONDON RECRUITING OFFICES
ALL BRANCHES OF
THE ARMY & SPECIAL RESERVE
ENQUIRE WITHIN
POLICE

The recruiting station at Scotland Yard, London, was besieged by would-be recruits during the first week of the First World War. The crowds were so large that mounted police were necessary to keep the gathering in check, 6 August 1914.

Despite the police presence, the queues were good natured.

Recruiting young soldiers in Manchester, August 1914.

Mobilisation of the Inns of Court Rifle Brigade, 6 August 1914.

Volunteers queue to enlist outside a recruiting office.

Russian infantry in Poland, making the long march to the battlefront, August 1914.

Russian leader Tsar Nicholas II looking through a periscope at the enemy positions, August 1914.

GERMANS SUFFER DEFEAT ON SEA AND LAND

BELGIUM ASKS FOR BRITISH FORCE

Germany has chosen to flout the mistress of the seas, and is even now paying the price. There have been rumours of battle in the North Sea, but so far there has been no confirmation of this.

Cannonading has been reported to have been heard off Margate, and it was reported from Dover that firing was going on all round, but there was no definite information.

Be this what it may, the British fleets are certainly harrying the Germans. Prizes of war and prisoners have already fallen into English hands.

A warship came into Dover yesterday with two prizes – a barque and a steamer. The richest prize yet is that of the *Belgia*, which ran short of coal and was later seized by armed police at Newport.

It smacks of the good old days, when rich prizes fell to the share of the British Navy.

Earl Kitchener, Sir John French, Sir J Grierson, Sir Alfred Codrington and several other general officers met at 10 Downing Street yesterday afternoon for a joint council. Mr Asquith and Mr Churchill, First Lord of the Admiralty, Prince Louis of Battenberg, the First Sea Lord, and Viscount Haldane were present. Naval officers also attended.

The King visited the Admiralty yesterday afternoon, it is understood for the purpose of conferring with the War Lords and War Staff. His Majesty motored from Buckingham Palace, and was attended by Sir Charles Cust. His arrival was almost unobserved by the public.

The Belgian Legation in London was informed yesterday by the Belgian Secretary of State for Foreign Affairs that the Government of Belgium had asked the British, French and Russian Governments for military assistance to preserve the neutrality of Belgium.

The police have issued notices at Hull that there may be firing practice off the Humber today and the inhabitants are warned not to be alarmed.

The Wilson liner *Novo*, from Stettin, reports that the Germans took out her cargo of sugar.

80,000 GERMANS REPULSED WITH HEAVY LOSS IN BELGIUM

A great German reverse was reported yesterday from Belgium,

THE DAILY MIRROR, Thursday, August 6, 1914.

BRITISH BATTLESHIPS HUNTING THE GERMAN FLEET.

The Daily Mirror

LATEST CERTIFIED CIRCULATION MORE THAN 1,000,000 COPIES PER DAY

No. 3,365. Registered at the G.P.O. as a Newspaper. THURSDAY, AUGUST 6, 1914 One Halfpenny.

FRANCE CAPTURES GERMAN CRUISERS WHILE THE BELGIANS REPULSE 80,000 OF THE INVADERS.

Dreadnoughts "on the roll" for home.

One of our recent battleships.

A Dreadnought showing her big guns in the bows.

There has been fighting by land and sea. The Belgians are making a stubborn and plucky resistance to the German advance through their territory, the invaders, it is reported, having been repulsed in a stubborn battle near Liege. There were 80,000 Germans, who were so harassed on the right that they had to retire. The Germans have, therefore, threatened to treat the Belgian peasants, who in any way hinder their march, without mercy. France has scored a naval success in the Mediterranean, telegrams stating that two German cruisers have been captured and the gunboat Panther (of Agadir fame) sunk. The pictures are of British battleships.—(Cribb.)

where fierce fighting took place on the outskirts of Liege. Eighty thousand Germans who tried to advance across Belgium into France were repulsed. The German losses are said to be very great.

News of a naval battle in the Mediterranean reached Paris, and the dramatic announcement was made that the German cruiser *Panther*, which caused the Agadir crisis, had been sunk.

French soldiers stand next to an aeroplane in a field in France.

HOLLAND – GERMANS CROSS THE MEUSE

Brussels, 5 August – The German Army has crossed the Meuse at Eysden in Holland, and the rattle of cannon can be discerned. It is said they are meeting with resistance.

RESTAURANT

Belgian civilians called up to bolster the line march off into action from Brussels, August 1914.

Amsterdam, 4 August – It is further reported that hussars are near Eysden, and that their object is to prevent German forces from proceeding through Dutch territory.

BELGIUM – 80,000 GERMANS REPULSED

Brussels, 5 August – A stubborn battle has been fought on the outskirts of Liege, where 80,000 Germans attempted to force their advance across Belgium.

They were engaged by the garrisoned troops of the Liege militia who, after a fierce encounter, so harassed the German troops on the right that they were forced to retire.

Belgian troops take up positions behind a barricade waiting for a German attack, August 1914.

BELGIUM – TOWNS IN FLAMES

Liege, 4 August – The Germans, hindered by the destroyed bridges, viaducts and railways, have been compelled to make for the north and have violated Dutch territory at Tilburg. They crossed the Meuse at Eysden.

The 10th Army Corps is said to be at Eysden, the 7th 40,000 strong at Verviers, and the 6th at a place unknown.

Vise and Argenten are in flames, the Germans having set fire to them.

Civilians are reported to have fired on the Germans, who are reported to have decimated the population of Vise.

GREAT GERMAN LOSSES

Amsterdam, 5 August – The efforts of the German invading force to repair the bridges have failed. Their losses are not yet known, but are undoubtedly very great.

The wounded German soldiers are being transported in automobiles to the Red Cross hospital at Maestricht. Up to the time of cabling, the Germans have failed to cross the Meuse or to capture the fortresses along the Belgian positions.

FRANCE – GERMAN CRUISER SUNK

Algiers, 4 August – It is reported that the French fleet has sunk the German cruiser *Panther*. Official intimation of this was received later at the French Embassy in London.

The Panther is the cruiser whose dispatch to Agadir nearly brought about a Franco-German war during the Morocco crisis.

A message from Guernsey stated that a French gunboat, with a large German steamer in tow, had arrived in Guernsey Roadstead and had anchored under the guns of the castle.

German soldiers in the field stop for a water break, August 1914.

RUSSIA – VILLAGES BURNT IN RETREAT

St Petersburg, 4 August – The Russian troops have established contact with the enemy along the greater part of the Russo-German frontier.

A reconnaissance has been made on the Bialla and Borzymmen front. The German troops have fallen back a day's march, burning the villages over an enormous stretch of the country.

RUSSIA – GERMAN FLEET IN THE BALTIC

St Petersburg, 5 August – A German squadron composed of 19 ships was signalled yesterday in the direction of Memel and Lihau. In the Black Sea, the Russians have captured several German merchant ships.

AUSTRIA-HUNGARY – AEROPLANE SHOT DOWN

Vienna, 4 August – The *Neue Freie Presse* publishes an account of the destruction of a Russian aeroplane by the Austrians on the Russo-German frontier north of Lemberg.

A Sikorsky aeroplane, with a Russian pilot and two Russian officers on board, was sighted by the Austrian troops, who immediately fired on the machine, bringing it crashing to the ground. Both officers were killed.

GERMAN SHIPS AS BRITISH PRIZES

NEWPORT POLICE, ARMED WITH RIFLES, SEIZE STEAMER WITH £200,000 OF FOOD

Many merchant German ships were seized as prizes yesterday. The German liner *Belgia*, from Boston to Hamburg, was taken as a prize at Newport.

The *Belgia* belongs to the Hamburg-America Line and anchored off Ilfracombe early in Tuesday morning, the captain coming ashore and attempting unsuccessfully to get into communication with the German Consul at Newport. He had run short of coal.

It is stated that the liner has a large amount of specie aboard consigned to Germany. It has over £200,000 worth of food on board, including 400 tons of cheese.

The police, armed with service rifles, boarded the vessel. On board there were a number of wild animals consigned to the Hamburg Zoo, including several large alligators. An armed guard has been placed over the vessel.

Lloyd's received a message from their agents at Dover yesterday to the effect that a British warship had seized two German vessels – *Perkeo*, German four-masted barque, and *Frans Horn*, steamer – and were coming into harbour.

The German ship *Terpsichore*, outward bound from Limerick, was seized yesterday by the authorities near Foynes, on the Lower Shannon. She belongs to Hamburg and had discharged a cargo of grain from Portland, Oregon.

In the Manchester Ship Canal at Warrington, the German steamer *Dryand* was taken possession of by the Custom House authorities. She was laden with timber from Sweden for Messrs Baylor Limited of Warrington.

Several foreign steamers are now under arrest at Hull. Any steamer entering the Humber is examined, and failing conformation to certain regulations is liable to be fired upon.

The German crews on the German steamers *Lucinda*, of Flensburg, and *Leuenson*, of Flensburg, are prisoners of war. The crews are not allowed to leave the ships.

The German Consul at Hull, who has been resident for 50 years in England, has left his duties.

Several German ships in Flyth Harbour for coal have been seized, and the crews placed under military guard.

GERMAN LINER TO GO TO WAR

New York, 5 August – The great Hamburg-American liner *Vaterland* is preparing to sail. She has on board no fewer than 8,000 German reservists and carries an enormous supply of coal.

All her staterooms have been converted into coal bunkers. The liner will be met at sea by a German warship, when she will be converted into a cruiser.

It is presumed that her extra coal will be used to supply the German warship.

PROPHETS WHO "TOLD US SO"

Seers, clairvoyants and mediums all over the country are claiming that they "forecasted" the great war months ago. Yesterday *The Daily Mirror* looked up the prophecies for August in *Old Moore's Almanack for 1914*.

There is no mention whatever of Germany, but Russia is frequently mentioned. "Our relations with Russia appear to be strained," says *Old Moore* in one piece. The prophecy goes on:

"Changes in the Ministry are shown about the 22nd of the month, and the vacation is likely to be disturbed by adverse events, in which the travelling public are involved.

"The 20th shows much excitement in financial circles and, having

regard to the current indications, I should judge that some warlike reports will come over from the East . . . the tone of the stock market will be weak.

"On the 21st the eclipse of the sun . . . during the month will be disturbing to France and Japan. Russia also may find difficulties confronting it in the Far East."

£100,000,000 AS SINEWS OF WAR

PAPER MONEY FOR ENGLAND – "ANYONE WHO WITHDRAWS GOLD IS HELPING THE ENEMY"

"I shall tomorrow ask for a vote of credit for £100,000,000."

Amid the sound of tumultuous cheering, which threatened never to die away, Mr Lloyd George, the Chancellor of the Exchequer, announced in the House of Commons last night that in Committee of Supply today he would ask for the above-mentioned sum.

The Chancellor also made the following momentous announcements with regard to the currency situation:

- ⋆ The Government will issue £1 notes.
- ⋆ Three million of the notes will be ready tomorrow morning.
- ⋆ Five million notes per day after that.
- ⋆ Until there is a full supply of £1 notes, postal orders to take their place.
- ⋆ All notes will be convertible into gold at the Bank of England.
- ⋆ Postal orders will be legal tender on the same terms as bank notes.
- ⋆ The Bank rate to be reduced to six percent today or tomorrow.

Among other arrangements that have been made are the following:

- ⋆ The Government are coining additional silver.
- ⋆ A Bill with regard to the issue of new notes will be introduced today.
- ⋆ The Moratorium will be greatly extended.
- ⋆ Arrangements are being made at the banks to furnish money for salaries, wages and other necessities of life.
- ⋆ Bankers consider themselves in a position to resume the normal course of business.

The Chancellor made a most earnest and impressive appeal to the public to refrain from withdrawing gold from the banks when they opened tomorrow. If they withdrew gold they would be inflicting great injury on the nation.

MONEY WILL TELL

In this tremendous struggle, finance was going to play a great part and it would be one of the most formidable weapons in this exhausting war.

If anyone withdraws more gold than he needs he will be assisting the enemies of his native land.

The House cheered in complete approval.

"I appeal to patriotic citizens," he added, "not to withdraw gold on Friday."

The Chancellor, moving to the adjournment of the House, announced that he had deemed it his duty to summon conferences of the leading bankers, merchants and manufacturers in order to confer as to the best way to meet the financial emergency.

The emergency, he assured the House, was "purely a temporary one, due to a temporary cause."

The Daily Mirror was yesterday informed by a leading Post Office official that during the last few days thousands of people have been presenting cheques at Post Office counters in payment of stamps.

Postmasters have no power to receives cheques in this way and it will save many fruitless visits to the Post Office if this is made plain to the public.

BLINDS DRAWN AT GERMAN EMBASSY

The German Ambassador, Prince Lichnowsky, leaves England this morning. Arrangements had been made a day or two ago at the German Embassy by the Ambassador and his staff for leaving London in the event of negotiations being broken off, and much luggage went on Monday and Tuesday.

Yesterday there were only a few formal calls for the Ambassador to make, and later several Ambassadorial representatives called and bade Prince and Princess Lichnowsky farewell.

The blinds of most of the windows at the Embassy are drawn. A

LIVERPOOL ST. 9
BANK CANNON ST.
LUDGATE HILL
STRAND CHARING
PICCADILLY
KENSINGTON ROAD
HAMMERSMITH RD.
9
LE-9315
BANK-CHARING
PICCADILLY
KENSINGTON-HAMMERSMITH
GENERAL
1301
WEAR
ARROW
all Hosiers
COLLARS
Iron Jelloids

workman removed the brass plate from the side of the entrance to the Embassy yesterday morning.

LONDON'S CHANGE TO CITY OF WAR

TROOPS THAT TOOK PASSENGERS' PLACES IN MOTOR-OMNIBUSES

The first day of war broke greyly over London. The great city itself was stern and calm. Throughout the day, from early morning until night, even when tremendous torrents of rain beat down upon the pavements, crowds of quiet citizens thronged the streets.

There was something massive in the attitude of these crowds, something set and reassuring. As a Frenchwoman remarked in the morning as she looked at the continual procession of men pacing Whitehall: "They look like a great army of plain-clothes policemen."

The general attitude was stamped with the semblance of responsibility. London, too, had been transformed into a martial city.

One saw soldiers everywhere, in twos and threes and in large companies, in trains and omnibuses and on bicycles. At Alexandra Gate a company of troops quietly held up the motor-omnibus traffic for a time.

First one omnibus and then another was stopped and the passengers requested to alight. None of them complained.

When a whole fleet of the vehicles had been collected the troops drove away to a destination which was not stated to the public.

Somerset House and all the other Government offices were under military guard. Amidst the sober black of the civilian population the bright gleam of a bayonet could be caught again and again.

Number 9 Omnibus carrying Territorials and loaded with ammunition leaving the powder magazine in Hyde Park, August 1914.

TAKING DOWN THE GERMAN EAGLE

A crowd gathered at the German Embassy and watched in silence the preparations that were being made in connection with the departure of the Ambassador. They were quiet and even respectful in their manner.

A single individual who attempted to "boo" was immediately stopped by the other members of the crowd before he was escorted away by the police.

A strange silence fell upon all those present outside the Embassy when a stolid-looking English workman quietly removed the brass plate emblazoned with the German Eagle from the front door. The man was characteristically methodical with his work.

He was almost irritatingly slow with the screwdriver. Some of the more ardent spirits in the crowd must have felt inclined to cry out "Wrench it off!" but no one spoke.

The groups stood round the workman in a sort of fascinated silence, watching history being made with a screwdriver!

When the crowd moved away from the Embassy they were confronted in Pall Mall by a body of mounted territorials escorting large numbers of remounts.

CALL OF THE BUGLE

Down the Haymarket some 30 or 40 sailors were being whizzed along in a grey motor lorry.

Somewhere in the neighbourhood of Whitehall a blast was being blown from a bugle. Two mounted guardsmen came galloping down the Strand. Veritably London had been transformed into a city of war!

At Whitehall a deep roll of cheers welcomed the arrival of General Grierson at the War Office. The general smiled in acknowledgement as he paused outside the War Office to give his horse and that of his orderly two lumps of sugar. Brigadier-General Sir Francis Lloyd was given another ovation.

So the grey old city itself went quietly about such business as there was on hand.

Green and chocolate uniformed men, with side whiskers and the faces of butlers, peered out discreetly from the half-opened doors of the banks and condescended, very magnificently, to buy one of the evening papers.

It seemed that large numbers of men had come to the City really out of habit or custom. There was actually no business for them to transact.

"THE STOLID ENGLISH"

So they stood together in groups on the pavements, read the newspapers, smoked and quietly discussed the situation.

London has shown a great deal more excitability over a football or boxing match than it manifested yesterday. The people justified their title as "the stolid English".

Nothing was more remarkable, nothing was finer than the attitude of the women. During the luncheon interval, when large crowds of women and girls poured out of the factories and shops, every onlooker remarked on the quietude of their attitude.

They bought the papers as eagerly as the men and discussed the situation in earnest whispers. But their tranquility, when one remembers the usual scenes of shrillness and laughter which take place daily at this hour of day, can only be regarded as miraculous.

BESIEGED BY RECRUITS

GREAT SCENES AT THE DEPOT IN ANSWER TO COUNTRY'S CALL

So great was the rush of would-be recruits at the central recruiting depot at New Scotland Yard all day yesterday that the besieged authorities had to send for the police.

The bombardment started early in the morning, when two converging armies of enthusiastic would-be recruits swept into either side of the yard and attempted to take the offices by storm.

The would-be recruits were described to *The Daily Mirror* by one of the most experienced recruiting sergeants in the service as being for the most part of excellent physique. He said:

"I have never seen better material in the rough. What classes are they drawn from? All classes – clerks, labourers, shopmen and youths who have just left school. After this rush we should have more "gentlemen rankers" in the Army than ever before."

The sergeant turned away. Two young men – one rough, ragged and unkempt; the other spruce, smartly clad and refined in speech – were buttonholing him.

One common cause had brought these two strangers together. They were besieging the sergeant together, and the eternal question which echoed round the recruiting offices all through yesterday was on their lips: "How can I join the Army?"

The call for recruits for the Hon Artillery Company also met with an astonishing response. No fewer than 300 joined on Tuesday, and yesterday men turned up at headquarters in overwhelming numbers.

Each recruit has to be nominated by a member of the company, and the staff was busily engaged in dealing with the huge number of applications for enrolment.

Another round of men queue to join the Army at Scotland Yard, London.

BOY SCOUTS ON GUARD

VIGIL KEPT OVER BRIDGES AND RAILWAY LINES – YOUNG BRITAIN MOBILISES

Boy Scouts all over the country are mobilising. There are 50,000 tough little Britishers ready and eager to help the civil and military authorities in every way they can.

Holidays have been abandoned, camps struck, pleasures and games abandoned in order to devote every minute of their time to the welfare of Great Britain.

Lieutenant-General Sir Robert Baden-Powell, the Chief Scout, has offered the War Office 1,000 scouts from each county to assist the Chief Constable in the following ways:

- Handing out notices to inhabitants, and other duties connected to billeting, commandeering, warning etc.
- Carrying out communications by means of dispatch riders, signallers, wireless etc.
- Guarding and patrolling bridges, culverts, telegraph lines etc against damage by individual spies.
- Collecting information as to supplies, transport etc available.
- Carrying out organised relief measures among inhabitants.
- Helping families of men employed in defence duties, or sick or wounded.
- Establishing first aid, dressing or nursing stations, refuges, dispensaries, soup kitchens etc in their club-rooms.
- Acting as guides, orderlies etc.
- Forwarding dispatches dropped by aircraft.

The Chief Scout has also offered the Admiralty 1,000 Sea Scouts to assist the coastguards in every way they can.

All over Sussex, Boy Scouts are guarding the railway lines, bridges, culverts etc at the request of the Chief Constable.

Boys themselves have been sending telegrams and letters begging to be allowed to do some useful work for the country. "Is there no work a King's scout can do at the moment for God, King and country?" runs one wire.

HOST OF "SPIES" ARRESTED

CHARGES OF ESPIONAGE AGAINST GERMANS ALL OVER THE COUNTRY

During the last 24 hours 21 spies have been arrested, chiefly important naval centres. This important statement, showing the keen vigilance of the authorities, was made yesterday afternoon in the House of Commons by the Home Secretary.

In London many houses occupied by Germans were raided, as a result of which four men – named Frederick Dredrich, Adolf

Scheider, August Klenden and Karl Erust – were charged at Bow Street under the Official Secrets' Act.

Dredrich, whose address was not given, said in reply to the charge of espionage: "I was a commander in the German Navy, but am now pensioned."

The Germans arrested in other parts of the country were:

Weymouth – Henry Schutte, a native of Hamburg, was remanded on a charge of obtaining sketch, plan, note and other documents and information calculated to be useful to an enemy.
Barrow – Frederick Appel, a German, was charged with contravening the Official Secrets' Act.
Penarth – William Fowler, a hairdresser, of Penarth, was charged with obtaining and selling information to Germany.
Sheerness – Frantz Losel, a photographer, of German nationality, was arrested by the military with a camera in his possession on a wall facing Sheerness Harbour, in which there were warships.
Falmouth – Johannes Engel, a ship's chandler, and a former lieutenant in the German Army was remanded, charged under the Official Secrets' Act.

Two men seen on the railway line between Cannon Street and London Bridge yesterday afternoon were taken to Cannon Street Station, where they were handed over to the police.

NO CHANCE OF FOOD FAMINE

HIGH PRICES IMPOSSIBLE IF PUBLIC BUYS NORMAL QUANTITIES

There can be no food famine. Under no conceivable circumstances in the immediate present can a wheat famine arise. High prices will not prevail if the public keeps its head, buys normal quantities of food, and refrains from making a panic rush on the provision merchants, in which case the eternal law of supply and demand will inevitably tend to raise prices.

The food supplies of this country have never been better than at the present moment. The supply of wheat is sufficient for four months' consumption. Other large consignments of wheat are nearing these shores.

We have ample supplies of grain, while our meat supplies are sufficient to last us for six months. Nothing can at present justify any rise in the prices of bread or meat.

NO PANIC – NO FAMINE PRICES

Nothing but a public panic can bring about famine prices, and for the most part the public is keeping cool. It should be noted, moreover, that the small shopkeeper is making no effort to reap a dishonest harvest out of the trials of his country. He is steadfastly refusing to raise prices except in the cases of those articles of consumption which have risen automatically.

Stern measures are being taken by the managers of London stores and the big shopkeepers to stop the absurd rush for huge quantities of provisions among certain Londoners during the past few days.

They are almost unanimously curtailing the amount of foodstuffs to be supplied to each individual. In some cases they have temporarily stopped business altogether – the grocery department of Messrs Spiers and Pond's stores was closed yesterday afternoon and will reopen today.

Small co-operative stores in the suburbs have almost unanimously decided to sell only certain quantities of provisions to their customers. Here, for instance, are the maximum amounts of foodstuffs being sold by the Edmonton Co-operative Stores:

- 7lb of sugar
- 1 pack of flour
- 7lb of rice
- 7lb of barley

The Civil Service Stores, Queen Victoria Street, have issued a notice that, "in consequence of the great demand for certain grocery and provisions, it is impossible to supply members for the present with more than the quantities of these articles corresponding to their ordinary requirements."

LIMIT SET BY STORES

At these stores people may not take away with them more than 2lb of sugar or one tin or bottle of each variety of meat or fruits. All biscuits have gone up 1d per pound, tinned goods 1d in the shilling, jam 1d per pound, and all cereals have risen in price.

"The ridiculous tendency among certain people to buy huge quantities of food must be stopped," said the manager to *The Daily Mirror*. "Please make it known to all your readers that it is quite unnecessary, and that there are plenty of provisions for everybody in the country.

"I should estimate that, even if not another ounce of food arrived in the country, there is enough stock of foodstuffs in London to last us all for at least three months." All the service revolvers in London

THE DAILY MIRROR, Friday, August 7, 1914.

H.M.S. AMPHION SINKS WITH 131 MEN.

The Daily Mirror

LATEST CERTIFIED CIRCULATION MORE THAN 1,000,000 COPIES PER DAY

No. 3,366. FRIDAY, AUGUST 7, 1914 One Halfpenny.

131 MEN PERISH IN WRECK OF BRITISH CRUISER: THE SHIP WHICH SENT GERMANY'S MINE LAYER TO HER DOOM.

Lieutenant J. C. Tovey. The ill-fated Amphion. She was launched in 1911. Captain C. H. Fox.

The Koenigin Luise, now at the bottom of the sea.

The launch of the Lance, which sank the mine-layer.

An official statement issued by the Admiralty last night announces that H.M.S. Amphion, a cruiser of 3,440 tons, struck a German mine and sank with the loss of the paymaster and 130 men. The captain and sixteen officers and 135 men were saved. It is also stated by the Admiralty that a line of mines had probably been laid by the Koenigin Luise prior to her being sunk off the Dutch coast about sixty miles from Harwich. The vessel which sent the Koenigin Luise to her doom was H.M.S. Lance, a new destroyer. Four shots sufficed to shatter her, the first taking away her bridge and the third and fourth tearing away her stern..—(Russell.)

have been bought up by the Government but a great supply will be forthcoming within the next few days, for our leading factories are working at the highest pressure to cope with the immense demand.

AUTOMATIC PISTOL BOOM

There was a rush on all the London gun shops yesterday for automatic pistols, and a huge business was done. Throughout the greater part of the day the police were busily occupied in issuing permits to the public for the purchase of pistols.

To get a police permit a householder must make a written declaration that he requires the weapon for the protection of his own house or is about to go abroad for a period of not less than six months.

The declaration must be signed by the applicant as well as by the police officer in the district in which the applicant resides, and the sale of the weapon had to be recorded by the firm in a book kept for the purpose.

An ordinary gun licence costs 10s.

DEMAND TO BECOME BRITONS

Large numbers of Germans still in England are seeking British naturalisation papers. *The Daily Mirror* learnt yesterday that several thousand Germans had applied to be naturalised.

Inquiries were made at the Home Office for confirmation where harassed officials, surrounded by excited groups of foreigners, remarked:

"We have no official information to communicate to the Press on the question."

That is the official statement, but the officials themselves made no attempt to disguise the fact that the demand for naturalisation papers at the present moment is absolutely unprecedented.

7 August **1914**

HMS *AMPHION* SUNK WITH THE LOSS OF 131 MEN

BRITISH CRUISER WRECKED BY GERMAN MINE: ADMIRALTY STATEMENT

It is with great regret that we have to announce that the light cruiser *Amphion* was yesterday struck by a mine. She sank with the loss of 131 lives. The saved include 17 officers and 135 men. An official statement was last night issued by the Admiralty as follows:

"HMS *Amphion* sunk this morning after striking mine. Paymaster G D Gedge and 130 men lost. Captain and 16 officers and 135 men saved."

The Secretary of the Admiralty issued the following statement at one o'clock this morning:

"In the course of reconnoitring after the minelayer the *Koenigin Luise* sunk this morning, the *Amphion* struck a mine. The fore part of the ship was shattered by the explosion, and practically all the loss of life ensued from this cause.

"All not killed by the explosion were taken off by the destroyers' boats before she sank. The captain, 16 officers and 135 men were saved. Twenty German prisoners of war who were confined to the fore part of the ship were killed in addition."

It was also stated by the Admiralty last night that a line of

mines had probably been laid by the German liner *Koenigin Luise* prior to her being sunk from Aldeburgh Ridge to Lat 52.10 N, Long 2.25 E.

Aldeburgh Ridge is only a mile off the Suffolk coast to the South of Aldeburgh. The line of mines indicated stretches northeast into the sea.

The *Amphion* was the flotilla cruiser of the Third Destroyer Flotilla, of 3,440 tons. It was unofficially reported at Harwich yesterday that the Third Destroyer Flotilla had been in action yesterday morning and that the result of the action was a British victory. No official confirmation was forthcoming last night.

500,000 MEN FOR ARMY

Britain has always opposed mine laying in shallow waters as a barbarous form of warfare. Details now to hand of the sinking of the German mine-layer *Koenigin Luise*, a passenger vessel of 2,183 tons, show that it was the new destroyer *Lance* that sank her with four shots. Twenty-eight German prisoners from the mine-layer are now at Shotley.

The British Army is to be raised by 500,000 men, on the application of Earl Kitchener, who has just been made War Minister.

Yet a further step in the European war of nations was announced last night in a message from St Petersburg that states Austria has declared war on Russia. It is officially denied that Italy has received an ultimatum from Germany.

Britain's naval campaign with France against Germany was discussed yesterday at the Admiralty, where French naval officers, who arrived in England at night by torpedo boat, sat in council with Mr Churchill.

◀ British soldiers and their horses on board ship on their way across the Channel.

▶ Russian infantry in trenches during their battle against the Austro-Hungarian Army on the Eastern Front, August 1914.

MINE LAYER SUNK IN SIX MINUTES

NEW BRITISH DESTROYER HERO OF FIRST ENGAGEMENT

The new destroyer *Lance* was the hero of Britain's first naval engagement in the war in sinking the *Koenigin Luise* off Harwich.

She only fired four shots. The first destroyed the enemy's bridge and the third and fourth tore away the vessel's stern. It is stated that

CHEERS FOR "BOBS" AT THE WAR OFFICE: GERMANY WANTS MORE POSSESSIONS

Lord Roberts was among the visitors to the War Office. The crowd quickly recognised the veteran Field-Marshal, and cheered him heartily.

Germany's chief overseas possessions are situated in the African Continent, and the map shows the position of her territories. They are large, but not as large as ours.

There was indeed quite a procession of famous soldiers to the War Office. The picture shows General Grierson leaving.

"Buy your colours now, gents," shout the hawkers, who are doing a fine trade in flags. A few people do benefit by a war.

Map showing German New Guinea. The empire is very anxious to add to her possessions and enable her surplus population to colonise and still live under the flag.

When the call to arms is sounded there is a great rush to serve the King. Recruiting stations all over the country are besieged by would-be soldiers, and at Scotland Yard mounted police are necessary to keep the crowd in check. The men belong to all classes. (*Daily Mirror* photograph.)

the *Koenigin Luise* sunk in six minutes. The British destroyer took the promptest measures to save those on board, and 28 prisoners are now in Shotley Naval Barracks. Many are suffering from terrible wounds. All were reported to be progressing as well as could be expected. None of the crew of the *Lance* received any injuries.

The German vessel was caught in the very act of laying mines about 60 miles from Harwich off the Dutch coast.

The town of Harwich is in a state of martial law and the principal buildings, in view of the landing of the prisoners, have been turned into hospitals and are flying the Red Cross flag.

The *Koenigin Luise* was a passenger steamer of the Hamburg-American Line of 2,183 gross tonnage and a speed of 20 knots. She was specially fitted for mine-laying.

SWEEPING SEAS FOR GERMAN PRIZES

BRITISH WARSHIPS' HAUL OF MERCHANTMEN – TWO BIG LINERS SEIZED IN HARBOUR AT FALMOUTH

The following captures of German merchantmen and liners were made yesterday:

* At Falmouth – HMS *Diana* brought into Falmouth the German three-masted schooner *Else* from Rio Grande with hides. The Hamburg-American liners *Kronprinzessin Cecilie* and *Prinz Adalbert*, which were lying in Falmouth Harbour, have been seized.

* At New Brighton – The battery fired across the bows of a passing barge which failed to obey an order to stop. A pinnace was sent out with a boarding party.

* At Greenock – The German steamer *Marie Glesel*, which left Barrow on Wednesday, was brought into Greenock, having been captured off the Isle of Man by a British warship.

* Off Wick – The German fishing lugger *Berlin*, of Emden, captured by the battleship *Princess Royal*.

* Off Malta – A German Levant liner has been captured by a British destroyer.

A German sailing ship from Hamburg has been brought into the Humber as a prize.

Paris, 6 August – A telegram from Ferryville (Tunis) states that the torpedo craft of the Bizerta floating defences have captured the German oil boat *Tsar Nicolas*, which was carrying 2,000 tons of oil to Mazut.

It is reported at Rio de Janeiro that HM light cruiser *Glasgow* has captured several German merchant vessels outside Brazilian waters.

GERMAN CRUISERS SUNK?

New York, 6 August – Captain Hersig, of the Uranium Line steamship *Uranium*, today informed British Consulate that he had intercepted yesterday wireless messages from the steamship *Lusitania* that two German cruisers, which had been pursuing the *Lusitania*, had been chased and sunk by British warships. The Admiralty state that so far they have no confirmation of this report.

The fishing smack *Loch Nevis*, of Lowestoft, reports having seen a naval encounter 40 miles to the southeast of Lowestoft on Wednesday afternoon. They state that the firing was but half a mile distant from them, and they say that a torpedo-boat destroyer, presumably German, was fleeing before two other warships, supposedly British, which kept up a heavy fire during the chase.

GERMANS LOSE 8,000 IN BATTLE OF LIEGE

TERRIFIC ONSLAUGHT AT ALL POINTS OF ATTACK

Deeds of valour that henceforth will live imperishable in the pages of history are being performed by the heroic defenders of Liege, the Belgian fortified town which a huge German army is making superhuman efforts to capture. Details of the fighting telegraphed yesterday say that:

* The Germans delivered a combined attack on the whole of the forts on the right side of the River Meuse.

* Their onslaught was terrific, but they were mown down and put to flight by a deadly hail of lead poured at them by the Belgian defenders, who displayed a magnificent dash and courage.

* The German losses are estimated at 8,000 killed and wounded. Seventeen guns were captured.

* Fadeless glory was obtained by a squadron of Belgian Lancers, every man of whom perished in a charge in which they killed 150 Uhlans.

ESSEN
FRIED. KRUPP

A Krupp heavy artillery gun loaded onto a railway truck in Germany, 1914.

Equally reckless daring was shown by a party of Uhlans who actually penetrated the heart of Liege in an effort to capture the military headquarters. They were surprised and annihilated.

It was reported in Paris yesterday that two of the forts had fallen before the attack of the Aix-la-Chapelle Army, and that through the gap thus made by the German light siege artillery the Germans were advancing on Liege.

RAKED BY LEADEN HAIL

Brussels, 6 August – Graphic accounts continue to be received here of fighting near Liege. At half-past 11 in the morning the German forces attacked Fort d'Archon, to the northeast of Liege, under the cover of their artillery.

The invaders crept up at the front, and the Belgians reserved their fire until the enemy, having come to close quarters, were preparing for the first onslaught.

Then, at a given signal, the Belgians let loose a perfect hail of lead upon the Germans, among whom terrible havoc was wrought by the machine guns.

Meanwhile Fort Chaudfontaine bombarded the enemy, some of whom took refuge in a chateau.

The Belgian artillery is said to have made excellent practice and the chateau was reduced in a short time to a mass of smoking ruins. The enemy retired all along the line.

One newspaper says that the German losses were between 4,000 and 5,000 and that the enemy abandoned 17 machine guns.

One squadron of Belgian Lancers, it is reported, was completely wiped out after killing 150 Uhlans in a desperate encounter, the captain dying at the head of his men.

A newspaper states that the Dutch troops opened fire upon the German fugitives who sought to cross the frontier.

Another account says that the Zeppelin airship, which was on its way to Liege, was struck by a shell fired from one of the forts near Battich and crashed upon the ground near the frontier.

A force of between 20,000 and 25,000 Germans passed through Manhay (Luxembourg) yesterday morning between seven and eight o'clock, marching in the direction of Aywaille.

MINE BLOWS UP TROOPS

Liege, 6 August – Several German howitzers are, it is reported, in position near Herve. Large German forces are lying in wait on the other side of the frontier. The Germans were repulsed in an attack upon the village of Rouesse.

The 10th German Army Corps, reinforced by cavalry, attacked Liege last night. The enemy had to cross some zones which had been mined. The mines exploded, and whole battalions of the enemy were killed.

Not a single fort has as yet fallen into the hands of the Germans.

Twelve hundred German wounded were picked up on the field of battle.

Six German officers disguised as Englishmen made their way at four o'clock this morning into the Governor's office. They were killed. The Governor is safe and sound.

UHLANS' LAST CHARGE

Liege, 6 August – Since half-past 11 o'clock last night the roar of gunfire continued uninterruptedly all round Liege. The Germans succeeded in forcing a way into the enceinte of the fort at Fleron directed their fire on Bressoux, where many houses were wrecked or burned down.

A detachment of Uhlans with unparalleled bravery succeeded in penetrating into Liege as far as the Rue Saints Pol, where the military headquarters are established, with the intention of seizing the latter, but they were fortunately surprised by our troops and killed.

Amid cries of "Long live Belgium", the Garde Civic sent out patrols in all directions, accompanied by buglers, announcing that the town had not been taken and that the army would continue to offer a brave resistance.

GERMANS IN FLIGHT

Brussels, 6 August – According to the Gazette, the alleged rout of the 7th Corps of the German Army during the fighting in Belgium is not confirmed in its entirety. The following, adds the paper, are the exact facts:

"The 11th Belgian Brigade, after having successfully driven back the attack of the 7th German Corps, pursued the fleeing Prussians with such energy that the general in command of the Belgians had to order our troops to stop and turn back.

"The enthusiasm of our troops was magnificent. A number of wounded Germans fled to Dutch territory, and it was this that gave rise to the belief that the enemy had been completely routed."

ALL INHABITANTS ARMED

"They suffered, however, considerable losses, which are estimated at 8,000.

"At three o'clock yesterday morning a fresh attack was expected, but nothing happened until some four hours later, when the 10th German Corps made an attack from the southeast on the Chaudfontaine and Boncelles forts. The enemy of the right bank of

the Meuse also began to bombard the Flemalle Fort, on the other side of the river.

"A fine resistance was made by the fort. It is hoped from the spirited defence offered that this fresh attack will be victoriously repulsed. The Belgians captured seven guns and are also stated to have made a number of prisoners.

"At Huy five Uhlans appeared before a bridge guarded by the Civic Guard. Firing ensued, in the course of which two of the Germans were killed and one was wounded. A fourth was captured.

"A German parlementaire again made proposals for the surrender of Liege, but the demand was met with a firm refusal.

"It is stated that a Zeppelin has come to grief in Holland. Firing has been heard in the neighbourhood of Maestricht."

PRINCE OF WALES JOINS THE ARMY

THE QUEEN'S WISH

The Prince of Wales, it was officially announced last night, is to be given a commission in the Grenadier Guards, and it is understood that he will go with them on active service.

It is known that the Prince, who joined the Navy and qualified for the rank of lieutenant, has been keenly anxious to prove his patriotism by serving King and country in the present grave crisis of the nation's history.

There is reason to believe that the Grenadier Guards will be quartered somewhere on the east coast.

The Prince's patriotism does not end with his desire for active services.

Simple but eloquent appeals to the people of England to contribute to the fund to relieve the distress inevitable in every great war were issued last night both by his Royal Highness and Queen Mary.

The appeal of the Queen is to the women of England, whose sympathies have been so deeply stirred by the knowledge that Her Majesty has a sailor son – Prince Albert – in the firing line in the North Sea.

"TO STAY DISTRESS"

The appeal by the Prince of Wales is as follows:

"All must realise that the present time of deep anxiety will be followed by one of considerable distress among the people of this country least able to bear it.

"We most earnestly pray that their suffering may be neither long nor bitter. But we cannot wait until the need presses heavily on us.

"A national fund has been founded, and I am proud to act as its treasurer.

"My first duty is to ask for generous and ready support, and I know that I shall not ask in vain.

"At such a moment we all stand by one another, and it is to the heart of the British people that I confidently make this most earnest appeal."

APPEAL TO WOMEN OF ENGLAND

The Queen has added the following appeal:

"A national fund has been inaugurated by my dear son for the relief of the inevitable distress which must be bravely dealt with in the coming days.

"To this end I appeal to the women of our country, who are ever ready to help those in need, to give their services and assist in the local administration of the fund."

LAST OF AMBASSADOR

GUARD OF HONOUR SALUTES PRINCE LICHNOWSKY AS HE BOARDS BRITISH SHIP

The German Ambassador, Prince Lichnowsky, left London early yesterday morning. There was no demonstration.

The suite left in motor-omnibuses and the Ambassador motored with his wife and a representative of the British Government in his private car to Liverpool Street.

The arrival at Harwich was marked by remarkable scenes.

A British cruiser was in waiting for the Ambassador, and as he passed to the vessel a guard of honour, composed of the Rifle Brigade, presented arms. The Ambassador crossed in a Great Eastern steamer. Prince Lichnowsky bowed in acknowledgement of the compliment.

BRITAIN FIGHTING EUROPE'S BULLY

MR ASQUITH AND THE "INFAMOUS PROPOSAL" OF GERMANY

"We are unsheathing our sword for a just cause." In this noble sentence the Prime Minister yesterday showed that Great Britain, true to her traditions, stood for Justice.

WHAT GERMANY COULD NOT BUY

In asking the House to agree to the resolution for £100,000,000 War Credit Vote, Mr Asquith said he did not think any statement made by Sir Edward was capable of answer, and certainly there had been no answer to the grounds upon which, with the utmost reluctance and infinite regret, the Government had been compelled to put this country into a state of war with a country which for many generations had been a friendly Power.

The papers which had been presented to Parliament would, he thought, show how persistent, even when the last gleam of hope seemed to have faded away, were the efforts of Sir E Grey to secure for Europe a lasting and honourable peace.

Proceeding, Mr Asquith dealt with the points in the document relating to the refusal of Germany to guarantee the integrity of the French colonies and the neutrality of Belgium.

He said if we had assented to these terms we should have given free licence to Germany to annex the whole of the extra-European dominions of France, and we should have been repudiating in a shameful way our obligations to Belgium.

The Belgians were fighting and losing their lives for the defence of their country.

What would have been the position of Great Britain today if, in the face of this spectacle, we had assented to the infamous proposal of Germany? What was this country to get in return for the betrayal of its friends and the dishonouring of its obligations?

We were to get a promise as to what Germany would do in certain eventualities – a promise given by a Power which was at that very moment announcing the intention of violating its own treaty and inviting us to do the same.

This war had been forced upon them.

What were they going to fight for?

They were fighting to vindicate a principle that the small nationalities should not be crushed in defiance of international good faith by the arbitrary will of a strong and over-mastering power.

Referring to Earl Kitchener's appointment as Secretary of State for War, Mr Asquith said that the new Secretary of State was not a politician, and the fact of his joining the Cabinet was in no way associated with politics.

On behalf of Earl Kitchener he asked for power to increase the Army by no fewer than half a million.

Both the Credit Vote and the Army increase were unanimously passed.

Lord Kitchener, Secretary of State for War, had been a career soldier and did not believe that the war would be over by Christmas 1914. Kitchener informed the Cabinet of his views. He believed that the war would last between three and four years and that the UK would have to mobilise millions of men to achieve victory. It was a remarkably accurate prophecy.

Your King and Country Need You

A CALL TO ARMS.

An addition of 100,000 men to his Majesty's Regular Army is immediately necessary in the present grave National Emergency.

Lord Kitchener is confident that this appeal will be at once responded to by all those who have the safety of our Empire at heart.

TERMS OF SERVICE.

General Service for a period of three years or until the war is concluded.

Age of Enlistment between 19 and 30.

HOW TO JOIN.

Full information can be obtained at any Post Office in the Kingdom, or at any Military Depot.

GOD SAVE THE KING

A batch of English nurses leaving Brussels for the front to tend to the wounded. The inhabitants gave them a splendid welcome, and everyone commented on how kind and sympathetic they looked, August 1914.

British troops asleep on Boulogne Quay, having just arrived to join their French and Belgian allies.

▲ Marching off to war, 1914.